ALL ROADS LEAD TO HOCKEY

All Roads Lead to Hockey

REPORTS FROM NORTHERN CANADA

TO THE MEXICAN BORDER

Bill Boyd

KEY PORTER BOOKS

Library and Archives Canada Cataloguing in Publication

Boyd, Bill (William T.)
All roads lead to hockey: reports from northern Canada to the
Mexican border / Bill Boyd.

Includes index.
ISBN 1-55263-618-6

1. Hockey—Canada. 2. Hockey—United States. 3. Boyd, Bill (William T.)—Travel—Canada. 4. Boyd, Bill (William T.)—Travel—United States. I. Title.

GV847.B62 2004   796.962'0971   C2004-902799-9

THE CANADA COUNCIL | LE CONSEIL DES ARTS
FOR THE ARTS | DU CANADA
SINCE 1957 | DEPUIS 1957

ONTARIO ARTS COUNCIL
CONSEIL DES ARTS DE L'ONTARIO

The publisher gratefully acknowledges the support of the Canada Council for the Arts and the Ontario Arts Council for its publishing program. We acknowledge the support of the Government of Ontario through the Ontario Media Development Corporation's Ontario Book Initiative.

We acknowledge the financial support of the Government of Canada through the Book Publishing Industry Development Program (BPIDP) for our publishing activities.

Key Porter Books Limited
70 The Esplanade
Toronto, Ontario
Canada M5E 1R2

www.keyporter.com

Text design: Peter Maher
Electronic formatting: Heidy Lawrance Associates

Printed and bound in Canada
04 05 06 07 08 09 6 5 4 3 2 1

This book is for my children, Adam and Pippa

Contents

Preface

SEVERAL YEARS AGO I was struck by a late-middle-age wanderlust coupled with a bewildering curiosity about hockey beyond what was being reported in the large Canadian newspapers and carried on national TV broadcasts. So, crossing the continent in fits and starts, I visited towns where I knew that hockey was or had been important, where it was still a community game and a family could afford to go to the rink without having to mortgage their home. I talked with players and coaches and old players and old coaches and fans, from Glace Bay, the once robust mining center on Cape Breton Island where hockey had been a state religion second only to Roman Catholicism, to Powell River. That's the mill town on the British Columbia coast whose isolation should have made hockey against the outside world a nonstarter, but whose determination and dedication saw that it didn't. And in places I went to where hockey was no longer played as it once was, there were still the stories about it that will last as long as hockey is played anywhere.

For this second book I went to fewer places, but spent more time in each of them. I began with a colorful piece of history—

the 1951 Barrie Flyers who, en route to the Memorial Cup championship, dramatically upset the Quebec Citadelles and Canada's finest junior player, Jean Beliveau. But besides its victory, that Flyer team also held the seed of tragedy: its best player, who was expected to star for years in the National Hockey League, wasted his talent instead and met a sad end.

After Barrie I went to northern Manitoba, cradle of so much good hockey, and later went to the devoutly Hispanic soccer country along the Texas–Mexico border. It may be too early to say whether the love affair with hockey down there will last, but there are, at present, more professional hockey teams in Texas than in any other state or province. In the older tradition, there was the historic rivalry between the University of Michigan and Michigan State. Finally, I drove to Fredericton to attend the Canadian university championships. St. Francis-Xavier, the small Nova Scotia school, won it all, principally because its coach tries to follow the best advice he says he ever received: "Make goddamn sure you get good players."

Besides Barrie, there were two other stops that didn't involve current teams. One was Warroad, Minnesota, where they love hockey as much as they do in Rimouski or Red Deer. Ever since I covered the Christian brothers, Bill and Dave, when they were playing for the U.S national teams in the sixties, I've been interested in their hometown. Regardless of Detroit's claims, Warroad is the real Hockeytown, U.S.A. "Hockey used to be like one big family in the U.S. and Canada," Bill Christian says. "Everybody knew everybody else. That was good."

Another stop was Harrisonburg, Virginia, to talk with the proud and profane and irrepressible John Brophy, the former Maple Leaf coach. Brophy spent more than fifty years in organized hockey as a player and coach. He's now retired, but he feels and talks as passionately about hockey as ever, and the Maple Leafs are still his team.

Something that particularly impressed me on my rounds was the devotion to the game of the coaches and the young players—whether in junior, minor pro or university. And there was the humor, self-deprecation and general politeness of the players that people who regularly cover sports tell me is often missing in other athletes. (Whether this "niceness" extends to most National Hockey League players, I have no idea.)

However, all this comes, like most things, with a caveat. There are those who think hockey is fine as it is; others sure as hell do not. The more common, but nonetheless angry, complaints often start with charges that players are greedy and spoiled and that owners do nothing except whine. Then there is the concern, sometimes expressed by the coaches themselves, that overcoaching—new systems and strategies—are strangling players' skill and creativity; and there is the growing fear that violence, sooner or later, will injure someone for life and that it is already reducing the most glamorous game in the world to clumsy football on ice. Everyone has a solution. Should ice surfaces be bigger? Should fighting be banned? Do face guards make players less responsible for their sticks?

(The research for this book was largely finished before Todd Bertuzzi's cowardly and stupid attack on Steve Moore and the later, bizarre situation that saw Mike Danton of the St. Louis Blues charged by the FBI with murder-for-hire. As well, as I write this, the collective-bargaining differences between the NHL and the players' association remain unresolved.)

For the most part, the same thing held true for this trip as for the earlier one: it was great fun, and although I'm sure there are jerks in hockey, as there are anywhere, I didn't encounter any. And in spite of all the qualifications about hockey today, I still feel that, at its best, it is the most demanding and exciting game in the world.

I would like to thank Brian Vallee, a fine writer, who acted as my agent in this case and placed my manuscript with Key Porter Books. I would also like to thank Meg Taylor, Key Porter's senior editor, for all her help, which made my job much easier, and Peter Maher, Key Porter's art director, for his imaginative cover. Thanks also to Lloyd Davis for an excellent copy edit.

CHAPTER 1

The 1951 Flyers and Chevy

BARRIE, ONTARIO • Jack Garner's good-natured face has a few nicks, which bear testimony to hockey before helmets and face masks. Jack is stocky with thick, grayish hair, yet he looks younger than his sixty-eight years. Until he retired recently, he ran Garner Sports in Barrie, Ontario, which his father, Bill, opened in February 1931 with $200 borrowed from the Royal Bank of Canada. The business is now run by Jack's son, John. It specializes in hockey equipment and is located on Dunlop Street, a few blocks east of the old Dunlop Street Arena. Dunlop used to be the busiest part of town, before shopping malls and big-box stores took over, and the Arena was the home of the first Barrie team to win the Memorial Cup, the 1951 Barrie Flyers.

In that dreary winter and early spring more than fifty years ago, a United Nations force, including the 2nd Battalion of the Princess Patricia's Canadian Light Infantry, was bogged down in Korea's snow and mud battling the North Koreans and the Communist Chinese. And as the Soviet Union and the West tried to face each other down in Europe, Americans were building nuclear fallout shelters in their backyards.

At home, Quebec's iron-fisted, church-backed premier, Maurice Duplessis, got into the act, blaming Communist sabotage when a bridge collapsed in his riding near Trois-Rivières, killing four people. Evidence later pointed to shoddy work by government-friendly construction companies.

Jack Garner was seventeen in 1951 and playing hockey in Toronto, an hour south of Barrie, for the Junior B Weston Dukes of the Ontario Hockey Association (OHA). The Dukes were the chief farm team of the Junior A Toronto Marlboros— OHA Junior A was then the highest level of junior hockey in the province—and the Marlboros, in turn, were run by the Toronto Maple Leafs. Garner's teammates on the Dukes included Billy Harris, the slim, classy center who later played thirteen years in the NHL, most of them with the Leafs, and Gerry James, the great Winnipeg Blue Bombers fullback and placekicker, who played parts of four seasons with the Leafs. (Of his own career, Garner says he might have made it as far as the AHL, but he had a chance to go to the Royal Military College in Kingston, so he took it.)

Over coffee a few doors down from the sports store, Garner looks back at the 1951 Flyers. "They were only a couple of years older than I was, but I idolized them," he says. "These guys were top-of-the-line juniors and anybody who knew anything knew that they were going to the NHL."

And they were right. Five of those Flyers, including the captain, Real Chevrefils, the most highly-rated junior in Canada that year after Jean Beliveau, became regulars in the National Hockey League. That's a remarkably high number to come from one junior team, particularly in the days of only six NHL franchises and the considerably smaller rosters they carried than nowadays.

Across Dunlop Street from Garner's Sports is Mike's Barber Shop, owned by fifty-five-year-old Mike Oliver, a tall, friendly man who knows all his customers and their families. It's a one-chair operation. "I'm on my own, cutting hair here and talking and telling lies for nearly thirty-five years," he says. In the shop, protected by Plexiglas, are a dozen or so photographs of the winning Flyers from the early fifties, their broad, open-mouthed grins showing lots of gaps and gums where teeth used to be. Mike Oliver got the photos from the family of Dooley Greer. "Dooley drove the Flyers bus," Oliver says. "He was also mayor. He knew I liked hockey. That's why I got the pictures."

Oliver was only five when the Flyers won their first Memorial Cup, but he does remember two years later, when they won their second. "Hockey was the social event of the week," he says. "We didn't have the malls, and the shopping wasn't open as late, so hockey was really important. It was where everyone went. Even now, people come into my shop and see those photos and want to talk about them. A lot of them have stories." He points to a picture of the team bus. "Like the team coming back from an away game. Dooley Greer not only drove the bus, he owned it and really looked after it. They say he drove pretty gingerly and slowly. The weather wasn't too good this night, but he's almost home. He's driving up a grade, in low gear, hardly moving. Apparently one of the players sneaks out the emergency exit at the back, runs up alongside the bus and pounds on the door. Dooley pulls over and opens the door and the guy starts panting and says, 'My God, Dooley, I thought I'd never catch you. You left me in Windsor.'"

Oliver still enjoys hockey. "There's not the finesse there used to be," he says. "Too much sticking for me, too much running at guys that don't even have the puck, but I still like to see the young players digging, playing hard. That's always good to see."

The Dunlop Street Arena, made of cement blocks with a rusting tin roof, has held more than 4,000 people when it had to, such as during its two Memorial Cup championship years. A dozen or so pennants hang from its rafters; the oldest is a tattered orange one that celebrates Barrie's Junior B Flyers, who won the Ontario championship in 1935. The rink is cold. It has hard, wooden benches and smells of mildew and sweat and chlorine and french fries, the smell that once marked small town rinks everywhere. The ice is good.

But the town of 12,000 in 1951, when the Flyers won that first Cup, has become a city of nearly 150,000 and has outgrown the old arena. It's now used for public skating, some figure skating, and hockey for youngsters and old-timers.

Barrie's current major junior team, the Colts, has a new home. The Barrie Molson Centre is in the city's south end, just off Highway 400, which leads north to "cottage country" and south to Toronto and is probably the busiest highway in Ontario, if not in the whole country. Glittering like a new penny, the Molson Centre has skyboxes and a restaurant and bar that overlook the ice. "It's a great place to watch a game," Mike Oliver says. "But a lot of the guys tell me that the ice at the Dunlop is still better. There's talk of them knocking the Dunlop down, getting rid of it, but I hate to think of that, all the history it's had."

Sam Cancilla, another Barrie native and businessman, was twelve when the Flyers won their first Cup. "It's hard to explain now how important hockey was then," he says. "I remember that even in July the newspaper would have stories on the Flyers and what they were doing for the summer. And when winter came, we couldn't always afford to go to the games, but we went to all the practices we could. It was magic for us."

In that spring of 1951, every Canadian over seventy became eligible for an old-age pension, pegged at $40 a month. There was no Canadian television, but 70,000 Canadian homes along the U.S border watched American TV. In sports, Joe DiMaggio was getting ready for what would be his final season with the New York Yankees and Willie Mays for his first with the New York Giants. Jaroslav Drobny, who had once played Olympic hockey for Czechoslovakia, would win the French Open tennis championship. And the Toronto Maple Leafs defeated the Montreal Canadiens in five games to win the Stanley Cup—all the games going into overtime.

But back in Barrie the attention of the young Jack Garners and Sam Cancillas—and the grown-ups, too—was on the Flyers' road to the Memorial Cup, hockey's biggest prize after the Stanley Cup.

The Flyers coach was Leighton "Hap" Emms, a Barrie native. He'd played more than eight seasons in the NHL and was considered big for his time, at six feet and nearly 200 pounds, and he was rough, taking his share of penalties. Off the ice, however, he was a devout member of the United Church and a stern moralist who now, as a coach, wouldn't allow his teams to play on Sundays.

"The players were well-behaved, decent young men," Jack Garner says. "Emms made sure of that. I saw them all the time.

They were always in and out of my dad's store. The team had an administration—directors and all that—but the bottom line was that Hap Emms *was* the Barrie Flyers and the Barrie Flyers were Hap Emms."

Leo Labine, one of the stars of that 1951 Barrie team and later a mainstay with the Boston Bruins, singles out Emms and two of his Bruins coaches, Lynn Patrick and Milt Schmidt, as the best. "Hap knew hockey inside out," Labine says. "He could be difficult—for one thing he was always fining me for swearing—but he made you want to play for him."

Until the 1990s, when Canada began to send its best players to the Olympics and other international tournaments, competition for the Memorial Cup captivated the country. Even today, with little interest shown in the Allan Cup, for senior hockey, and the falling off of football's Grey Cup, the Memorial Cup is the last true sporting event that unabashedly pits one region against another—Quebec and the Atlantic Provinces vs. Ontario vs. the Prairies and the west coast.

Named to honor the Canadian dead in the First World War, the Memorial Cup was first played for in the spring of 1919. The University of Toronto Schools won it, handily defeating the Regina Pats. And judging from what may have happened as UTS advanced towards that final, winning may have been as important then as later, when the Cup became established.

According to Richard Lapp and Alec Macaulay in their fine book, *The Memorial Cup*, there were charges not only that someone had put pepper and itching powder in the jockstraps of the Woodstock team that UTS defeated in the 1919 semi-final, but that the Woodstock skates had been meddled with.

This, reportedly, was related to heavy gambling on the series. Since then, itching powder or not, the Cup has been won by teams ranging from Montreal, Toronto, Winnipeg and Ottawa to Flin Flon, Manitoba (population 7,500), and Rimouski, Quebec. Even the Americans have won it: the Portland Winter Hawks, in 1983 and '98, and the Spokane Chiefs (both teams play in the Western Hockey League), in 1992.

The sun is streaming in through the windows of the spacious apartment in North Bay where Leo Labine, the old Boston Bruin, lives with his wife, Rosemary. North Bay is about an hour south of Haileybury, which is hard by the shores of Lake Timiskaming, and the place where Labine was born. "This has always been my part of the country," Labine says. "Except for when I was playing, I've never really thought of living anywhere else."

He was among the scores of young men who came out of the Northern Ontario mining region in the thirties, forties and fifties—and are still coming—to play in the NHL, ranging from Toe Blake through Ted Lindsay, Tim Horton, Dick Duff, Frank and Peter Mahovlich to Ron Duguay and today's Dave Lowry, Todd Bertuzzi and Steve Sullivan. Blake played thirteen seasons for the Canadiens and then coached them to eight Stanley Cups; Lindsay, of the Detroit Red Wings, was the NHL's best left winger in the late forties and fifties and was instrumental in establishing the players' association; Horton, a defenseman, was a leader of the great Maple Leafs teams of the sixties that included Duff; the Mahovliches, between them, played thirty-four NHL seasons; Duguay, a flashy crowd favorite, was a high-scoring winger for the New York Rangers and Detroit in the seventies and eighties.

Labine was a right winger and, at seventy-one, is not much over the 175 pounds he carried through his hockey career. His hair is snow white, but the tell-tale bent nose gives a lot away, and he still has all the nervous energy that made him one of the of the most focused and fiery—some say dirtiest—players of his time. Over his ten-plus NHL seasons he scored 139 regular-season and playoff goals and assisted on more than 200—and this was when a season was seventy games rather than the eighty-plus of today and the playoffs were made up of two best-of-seven series, half what they are now. He also took nearly 900 penalty minutes. "But before I even got up there I was missing four teeth," he says. "I lost two playing juvenile and two in junior. Then I got hit and my eye teeth came right through my lip."

To talk about hockey today, Labine has had to give up a golf game, but he doesn't seem to mind. He's having fun, jumping up and down from his chair like an excited kid, producing scrapbook after scrapbook. Photographs and newspaper clippings and pages of statistics spill out of them. And all the while he's talking, talking nonstop, barely finishing one story before he's starting another.

"Barrie Flyers Eastern Champs" was the front-page headline in the *Barrie Examiner* on a spring day in 1951 after the Flyers defeated the Quebec Citadelles 8–3 in front of 15,000 fans at Maple Leaf Gardens. That meant they had won the series four games to three and qualified to play in the Memorial Cup final against the Winnipeg Monarchs.

The victory over Quebec was particularly sweet. The Citadelles not only had the great Jean Beliveau, they also had

Camille Henri (who later anglicized his surname to Henry). A slick player, difficult to check, particularly in front of the net, "Camille the Eel" played thirteen seasons in the NHL, twelve of them with the New York Rangers, scoring nearly 300 regular-season and playoff goals. The Citadelle goalie, Marcel Paille, also became a Ranger.

Beliveau, in his autobiography written with Chrys Goyens and Allan Turowetz, says that the Citadelles might have won it all that year if Frank Selke Sr., the Montreal Canadiens general manager, had allowed Dickie Moore to play for them. In those days teams could pick up one or two players from their own league for the Memorial Cup playoffs. But because of squabbling within the Canadiens organization, Selke refused to let Moore, a member of the Junior Canadiens, join the Citadelles.

Moore played fourteen NHL seasons, twelve with the Canadiens; he won two scoring championships, was a member of six Stanley Cup teams and was named to three All-Star teams. After hockey he built a successful company that sells and leases construction equipment—it's difficult to walk around Montreal or Toronto without seeing his cranes and bulldozers and portables on building sites. But in spite of all that, he can still get steamed up about that Memorial Cup more than fifty years ago.

"Selke said I'd be a traitor if I played for Quebec," Moore says, "I said they're both Quebec teams and we're playing Ontario, and Selke said it didn't matter. He told me if I played for the Citadelles he'd see I never played hockey again."

But, Moore or no Moore, Beliveau concedes that "Barrie was a powerhouse."

Sam Cancilla remembers it well. "All the newspapers said how Quebec was going to chase poor little Barrie right out of the rink," he says. "With big Jean they were meant to take us easily. There was some terrible stuff here—anti-French, anti-Quebec name-calling. It was just awful. There was so much animosity towards the Quebec team. I'm not saying that being anti-French, anti-Quebec was right, but the Orange Lodge [the Protestant fraternal order] was powerful then, and this was a conservative area to begin with, so looking back it wasn't surprising. And it wasn't just anti-French: St. Mike's would get a hard time because they were Catholic."

Not only that, but Camp Borden, one of Canada's largest military bases, is near Barrie, and fifty years ago memories of the Second World War were still fresh. "This was an army town, so there was a lot of resentment towards the French from that angle, too," Cancilla says. He's referring to the reluctance of many Quebecers to enlist, and their sometimes violent opposition to any form of conscription. Led by the church, they saw the war as a European one, one that Canada should stay out of. Cancilla points out, however, that the Flyers had French-Canadian players and they were welcomed. "Mind you, they didn't come from Quebec. Most of them came from Northern Ontario."

"Yeah, Emms loved to get guys from up north like me and Topper, and Chevy and Mohnsy," Labine says, meaning Jerry Toppazzini, Real Chevrefils and Doug Mohns.

The series against Quebec went seven games, with Barrie's "home" games to be played in Maple Leaf Gardens and in the Dunlop Street Arena. "Sure, the league didn't like the Flyers playing at the Dunlop—they wanted the big gate receipts in

Toronto—but it was only fair to all the fans here," Cancilla says. "It was Barrie's team, not Toronto's. We jammed our place—more than 4,000 people."

The Citadelles won the sixth game in Quebec, tying up the series and setting the stage for the seventh and final game before a crowd of nearly 14,000 at the Gardens. The Citadelles opened the scoring, but the first period ended 2–2. Then the Flyers took command and won going away, 8–3. Labine had two goals. Morrison and the multitalented Chevrefils also scored. Afterwards, Emms told the Toronto *Telegram* that Chevrefils "night in and night out gives us everything. When he's on the ice the pressure is on the enemy because from the blue line in he can score. He can set up plays. You can't relax for one second or he's gone and it's a goal."

Chevrefils, with still another year of junior eligibility, had scored 52 goals and 103 total points over 54 games through the 1950–51 regular OHA season. Toppazzini, from Copper Cliff, Ontario, near Sudbury, scored 90 points and Labine scored 78.

Jim Morrison, a Barrie defenseman in 1951, came from Montreal. He was a superb skater who spent twelve years in the NHL, breaking in with Boston but playing most of his career in Toronto. "We had a heck of a good team," he says. "But what was really important, too, was that we were a close team. A lot of good-natured guys."

"Like most people, I was surprised they won," says Jack Garner, who saw that final game. "But it just goes to show— and it's happened before and it'll happen again—a team of sixteen solid players can beat a team built around a star."

Don Emms, a nephew of Hap Emms, was on that Barrie team. "I remember everywhere Beliveau went, Don Emms went," Garner says. "Emms wasn't there to play offense, he wasn't there to play defense. He was there to neutralize Beliveau, and he did. And Beliveau was big, well over six feet and 200 pounds. Emms was just a little guy compared to him, but he drove him nuts." The next day, the *Barrie Examiner* referred to Beliveau's frustration with the close checking. It reported, "Following the game . . . all the players but Beliveau remained on the ice to shake the hands of . . . the Flyers, who definitely won a moral and solid championship when all the odds were stacked against them."

It went on, "The victory celebration actually started in front of Maple Leaf Gardens as the Flyers filed to the bus. Hundreds remained after the game to congratulate the lads who fought tooth-and-nail . . . On the road home a stream of cars stretching bumper-to-bumper for three or four miles followed the Flyers' bus and as each town was passed, citizens were on the streets waving to the new titleholders."

By coincidence, an old Citadelle, Ray Cyr, settled in Barrie after his hockey was over. Cyr says that Phil Watson, the long-time New York Ranger and later the Ranger coach, scouted him at a high school tournament in his native New Brunswick and signed him for the Citadelles. "I was just a kid for that series against Barrie and didn't get much ice time," he says. "But I still remember they had two guys on Beliveau. He was far and away our best player, but he was going nowhere."

Cyr, a center, spent his career largely in the old Western Hockey League, a minor league on a par with today's AHL. He then returned to the east as a player-coach, first with a senior team in St. John's, Newfoundland. He says that Howie Meeker, the ex–Maple Leafs player and then coach (1956–57) and later hockey's premier TV analyst, played defense for him. "I think he was forty-five or forty-six," Cyr says. After St. John's, Cyr ended up with the Barrie seniors.

He still wonders occasionally at the turn his career took. "Watson wanted me to sign with the Rangers, and Punch Imlach wanted me to sign with the Quebec Aces of the old Quebec league," he says. "I didn't know which way to go, so maybe I went the wrong way when I signed with the Rangers and they sent me to Vancouver. Maybe I'd have had a better shot at the NHL under Punch, but that's something I'll never know." He says that he was on six championship teams over his professional career. "But I hated missing out on that Memorial Cup. I'll never forget that."

Ten days after beating Quebec, the Flyers, in what was almost an anticlimax, polished off the Winnipeg Monarchs to win the Memorial Cup. The series was split between Winnipeg and Brandon, and the Flyers took it in four straight games. Two days later, the *Examiner*'s headline read, "Despite rain, residents of Barrie and district turned out 10,000 strong to welcome home the junior hockey champions of Canada."

"Heck, our population then was only about 10,000," Cancilla says. "We had farming and some light manufacturing, and General Electric had a plant here, but the town was nothing like today. I remember relatives from California coming up and saying, 'Y'know, Barrie is four blocks long and four blocks wide.'"

The *Examiner* also reported that "Mr. and Mrs. Clarence Allen of Newmarket continued their record of not missing many, if any, games in the six seasons of Barrie hockey. They could not get away until Friday and then started out by car. A broken spring held them up in the States and they arrived too late for the third game in Brandon. But they were on hand for the championship game."

Besides Labine, Morrison and Chevrefils—although Chevrefils's career was cut tragically short—that Barrie team sent Toppazzini and Mohns, who also played for the Flyers team that won the 1953 Memorial Cup, to the NHL. Toppazzini scored 407 points, including 163 goals—plus 13 in the playoffs—over twelve seasons, most of them with Boston. Mohns lasted an amazing twenty-two seasons, largely with Boston and Chicago, playing forward and defense.

A headline in the 1957 Toronto *Telegram* acknowledges Barrie's contribution. "Barrie Takes Bow for Success of Bruins," it says over pictures of Labine, Chevrefils, Toppazzini, Mohns and Don McKenney. McKenney played for Barrie's '53 Memorial Cup champions; Jim Morrison had by this time been traded to Toronto. (Probably only Guelph, which won the Memorial Cup in 1954, sent as many players—Andy Bathgate, Ron Stewart, Harry Howell, Dean Prentice, Ron Murphy, Bill McCreary and Aldo Guidolin—on to distinguished NHL careers.)

"Some of the players on those fifties teams were billeted near where I lived and we'd be playing road hockey and down the street we'd see Mohns or McKenney coming," Cancilla remembers. "They'd yell, 'Got any extra sticks?' and of course we would, and they'd play with us. Orval Tessier, who was a helluva goal scorer, would play, too. But the best was Jerry Toppazzini. That guy was so intense. He loved any competition."

Cancilla says that Red Storey, the veteran on-ice hockey official and a Barrie native, had called Toppazzini probably the best penalty killer he'd ever seen. This was after Toppazzini had scored 7 shorthanded goals in one season, a record at the time. "And I can see why, because of that tremendous intensity. Even in road hockey." Cancilla pauses. "And then we'd see them downtown on a Saturday night, heading for the pool hall or a movie, all smartly dressed, overcoats with the collar up— you always had the collar up in those days—and in fedoras or porkpie hats and snappy pants. We wanted to be just like them. They were our heroes."

Hap Emms could be as unpredictable and difficult to play for as his contemporary, Eddie Shore, the ex–Boston Bruins great who was a coach, minor-league team owner and maddening eccentric. Jim Morrison says he was once benched and never understood why. "Emms wasn't playing me much then, and in one game when he did, the goalie goofed and I scored, on my first shift, and this seemed to make him even madder because I'd barely been on the ice. He didn't play me again, and after the second period he told me to take my stuff off. All he said was 'I don't want you here.' Although we made it up later, I never did figure out what I'd done wrong. He never mentioned it again.

"But I learned more from him than almost any other coach. He used to stress the importance of waiting for an opening to make a play. Another thing we worked on was moving the puck out of our end. I know all this sounds obvious, but he worked us hard and you see a lot of hockey teams out there now who've still never learned it."

Emms coached four Memorial Cup winners—the Barrie Flyers in 1951 and '53 and, after he moved the team there, the Niagara Falls Flyers in 1965 and '68. His Niagara Falls players included Bernie Parent, Derek Sanderson, Don Marcotte, Jean

Pronovost, Rosaire Paiement, Rick Ley, Brad Selwood and Gilles Marotte, all of whom had successful NHL careers.

"He was great to play for," says Marotte, a defenseman who played twelve NHL seasons for five teams, including the Bruins and the Rangers. "He was really tough, really strict, but he was fair. He'd turned out so many NHLers over the years that you knew he had to be doing something right. It was with him that I began seriously to think I had a shot at making the NHL."

Labine says, "Emms was always on top of things. Nothing got past him. One thing he'd do is pull you off the ice if you'd scored a goal. If the next line scored, he'd pull them off. He did that to remind us that hockey was a team game, not a one-man show. Another thing Emms wanted was to make sure, if one of their guys was coming out of his end, to make him come out on his backhand side so he'd probably have to turn to make the pass. You come in on his other side and he can rifle the puck around the boards." (However, this coaching touch didn't travel well. When he was briefly GM in Boston, Emms tried to switch Bobby Orr from defense to get more scoring up front. It didn't work.)

Sam Cancilla says he was told that when the Flyers went to play in Maple Leaf Gardens, which was owned, along with the Leafs and the Marlboros, by the combative Conn Smythe, Emms would insist on being given the lousiest dressing room. "Then he'd tell the team that the Gardens had all kinds of good dressing rooms but that Smythe hated Barrie so much, this is what he gave them. He'd get them so psyched up they'd take on anybody."

Jim Morrison hadn't heard the dressing room story, but he says he wouldn't be surprised. "With Emms, anything was possible. All the dressing rooms for the minor-league clubs at the Gardens were cubbyholes, but I wouldn't put it past him. He'd do anything to get an edge."

Morrison, the Montrealer, is seventy and, like Labine, looks in playing shape. After his twelve NHL seasons, he scouted for Boston for eighteen years. This morning he's sitting in a coffee shop in Barrie, a few miles from his new home in Wasaga Beach. He says he got out of the house for a while because they're laying the floor in the kitchen. "I was about sixteen when I decided I might have a shot at a career in hockey," he says. "I certainly had all the ambition you'd ever want. I'd be on those outdoor rinks for hours, all by myself, working away—skating, shooting, puck handling."

He was with the Verdun juniors in Montreal's system—although he didn't belong to the Canadiens—when Boston signed him and sent him to Barrie for the 1950–51 season. He joined the Bruins the next year, but halfway through it he was traded to Toronto for Fleming Mackell. "In my second year with the Leafs I scored nine goals and had eleven assists and was way up on the plus side of the plus/minus," Morrison says. "Hap Day was the GM and I asked him for a raise. By the time he was finished with me I felt I was lucky to even be playing in the league.

"But I wasn't really a defenseman. I was a strong skater, and I think the emphasis on defense may have hurt my game. In Toronto, under Day, all he wanted the defense to do was shoot the puck in and let the forwards chase it. If we didn't throw it in we were fined, $50 a crack. We weren't making anything like the money they do today, so after 200 bucks or so I said the hell with it and did what Day wanted.

"I remember playing Detroit, and every time he was on the ice Alex Delvecchio would just wait back there and skate the puck out. We might just as well have handed it to him on a plate. I had a big argument with Day about it, but it didn't do any good."

Of that 1951 Barrie team, Morrison says, "I guess the best memory is beating Quebec, with Beliveau, in that eastern final game before that huge crowd in Maple Leaf Gardens. That's something you'll never forget. Then we took Winnipeg four straight. There's nothing like it when you're young."

The Flyers were Leo Labine's second junior team. He'd had a good year with Toronto St. Mike's, so Emms went after him. "When you're the best junior team in the country it's easy to get players," Labine says. "Hap was way ahead of his time. George Steinbrenner goes out and buys players for his Yankees and everybody gets excited. Emms was doing that fifty years ago. He bought me for a year, and Morrison, Lorne Howes, George Stanutz . . . and after we left he brought in other guys."

The next year, after a short spell with the Hershey Bears in the American Hockey League, Labine began his eleven NHL seasons—nearly all with Boston. He still has a handwritten letter from Lynn Patrick, the Bruins GM, apologizing for having to trade him to Detroit. He also has circulation problems in his hands. "I broke them both," he says, holding them up. He says he took a swing at Dickie Moore with his right, missed him, and hit Moore's teammate Henri Richard. "They should have pulled it out, straightened it out, but all they did was freeze it and tie it," he says. He holds up his other hand. "This wasn't a fight. I think a guy gave me a two-hander.

"Certain guys you could fight, but you didn't go looking for someone like Gordie Howe," Labine says. "I said something one night that Howe didn't like, and he punched me in the mouth. As I'm going down I swung my stick at him. I got thrown out of the game for intent to injure, and he got nothing. That's the breaks when you take on the guy at the top of the ladder . . ."

Labine laughs and tells a story about the NHL's most gentlemanly player award. "We're in Montreal at the start of the season. Red Storey's refereeing, and we're facing off, and I looked up and said, 'Red, I'm going after the Lady Byng this year.' He just shakes his head. 'Leo,' he says, 'you won't get through your third shift without a penalty' . . . I think he was right."

Labine pulls out a photograph of some of the Bruins. "There's Topper, Mohnsy, Vic Stasiuk, Horvath—Bronco could sure put the puck in the net—and me. We got along well together, in Barrie and in Boston. When you have Milt Schmidt as captain, and later Eddie Sandford, it's hard to miss. We had a lot of respect for our captains, coaches, management and the news media."

Another newspaper clipping falls out of a scrapbook. It's from his days with the Los Angeles Blades of the old Western Hockey League, after he'd left the NHL. Leo Labine, the newspaper says, "is one of the most penalized players in the sport."

Labine tells a story about playing against Bill Ezinicki, the one-time Maple Leaf. They were both in the AHL, on their way up—Ezinicki with Pittsburgh and Labine with Hershey. Like Labine, Ezinicki wasn't very big, but he was one of the hardest open-ice bodycheckers wherever he played and an all-around tough guy. "I always figured it's better for me to hit you than you to hit me," Labine is saying. "So we're playing, and I hit Ray Timgren, who wasn't hard to hit, and I'm in the penalty box and I'm yapping away. Ezinicki skates by, and I called out, 'You might scare some of the guys out there, but you don't scare me.' I stuck my head out like Woody Woodpecker in the cartoons and Ezinicki decks me, really lets me have it.

"Johnny Crawford was our coach. When I got back to our bench he said, 'Jesus, Leo, you don't do that to guys like him. You never know what's going to happen.' He was right. That's what I get for yapping, not paying attention. You gotta pay attention if you want to last in hockey. I learned that in a hurry."

Ezinicki, later a teammate of Labine's briefly with the Bruins, is a golf professional near Boston. "He was a good guy to have on your side," Labine says. "Besides, I got my golf clubs from him."

Labine still follows hockey but, like a lot of his generation, he often doesn't like what's happening to it. "The other night, in the last couple of minutes, Carolina kept icing the puck. They'd win the face-off, then ice the puck. But one time they lost the face-off, there's a scramble and Dallas scores. Stupid hockey. Carolina had control of the puck and if they hadn't iced it they could have had the puck at the other end. You fight like hell to get the puck, then you give it away. Doesn't make sense.

"And there's too much interference. They're running guys who are nowhere near the puck. Every year the officials say they are going to crack down on it, but they never do. I sometimes think the people in charge of hockey don't really give a damn about it. I mean it. They sure as hell don't act as if they do. Either that or they're dumb as hell."

Labine looks down at his scrapbook, and then up again. "Y'know what my biggest thrill in hockey was? To be able to play in that league, play in the NHL, to make it to the top. And

I certainly wasn't the worst player on the team. I always carried my load."

Bill Hagan, who at seventy-one is as tanned and fit as Labine, was one of the few Barrie natives on that 1951 Flyers team. He later played minor professional hockey—for Buffalo and Vancouver before both cities entered the NHL—and senior amateur, for Owen Sound and Collingwood. Then he was off to Saudi Arabia for fifteen years with an American construction company. "It was great," he says. "I traveled all over Europe and most of the rest of the world. But by the time I got back I was too old even for old-timers'."

Not surprisingly, he says winning that Memorial Cup was the highlight of his hockey career.

The *Barrie Examiner*, in a special Memorial Cup edition, looked back on an important game against the Toronto Marlboros as the Flyers' regular season wound down. First place in the OHA was at stake. "Well, the game is now history," the newspaper said, "as Barrie polished off the junior Maple Leafs 7–0 in one of the roughest contests seen in years. Barrie's Bill Hagan was smashed into the boards by Marlie Ron Hurst. Hurst was given a match penalty and suspended for four games. Hagan is in hospital with a concussion and a ten-stitch head cut."

"I had a dislocated shoulder, too, so I was out for a while," Hagan says. "When I came back they made me wear a helmet, and in those days helmets were pretty lousy, just a piece of leather front and back. Besides, a helmet made you a marked man. I didn't want to wear the damn thing, but Emms made me. It's funny the things you remember."

Hagan says his only regret is that there wasn't more help in planning a career when he was young. "It was a different time," he says. "I remember when I made Buffalo [the Bisons, then in the AHL], it was the greatest thing that ever happened to me. I never thought about the future. I just thought that things were going to carry on.

"But I loved playing for Emms. He instilled something in you. I don't know what it was, but you'd want to go through the end of the building for him. He was very hard on you. He demanded the best. I remember in those days coaches insisted you keep both hands on the stick. If you didn't, Emms would tape your hands right to the stick and you'd play the whole practice that way. He was an interesting man. He could rip you up and down—he never swore. 'Gol'darn' was his favorite expression—but he never held it against you."

Doug Mohns says, "Emms was the one who developed my talent and skills. He was a real disciplinarian. We didn't like it at the time, but we appreciated it afterwards."

Hap and Mabel Emms' only child, Paul, was on that 1951 team. "My dad was honest. He'd do exactly what he'd say he'd do. There was no fooling around. He'd make his point and we'd accept it. For me, I tried to be as loyal as I could to the family, to him, but on the other hand, if I knew there was something going on with the players, I couldn't go back and tell Dad. Don't get me wrong. There wasn't that much, but you'd hear little things now and then and you'd try to ignore them."

Paul Emms says his father struggled hard to resolve the question of playing on Sunday. "He believed the players should have a day off," he says. "He went to ministers and to the players' families about his beliefs because he wanted their input, and as far as I know they all supported him. But it was shot down and we started to play on Sunday. Dad didn't try to stop the players, but he wouldn't have anything to do with it himself." When Emms lost his fight, Bill Long, his assistant coach, handled the team on Sundays.

Jack McKnight, who was on that team, isn't so sure about Emms' motives. He points out that Conn Smythe naturally wanted to see his Maple Leaf Gardens packed on a Sunday. "I know Hap didn't like playing on Sunday, but I think some of it was a 'screw Toronto, screw Smythe' attitude," McKnight says.

Jack Garner agrees. "There was a lot of rivalry, even dislike, between Smythe and Emms. Maybe Hap was a bit jealous. He'd have loved to have had the influence in hockey that Smythe had."

Whatever his motives, McKnight calls Emms a great coach. "He liked tough hockey. He never told us to go out and maim someone, but he wanted them roughed up. He wanted them to know they'd been in a game."

He goes on, "Leo kept the team loose. I remember one night Hap had him checking their best player, whoever it was. He told him to stick right with him, no matter what. Leo does such a good job that their guy's getting less and less ice time because he can't do anything when is out there. This means Leo's getting less ice time, too, because the guy's his assignment. Finally, about halfway through the third period, Leo skates over to the other coach and complains. He tells him to play the guy more so *he'd* get some more ice time.

"I guess we all got around $40 a week. Maybe Leo got a bit more and Chevy around $75. Chevy was something else. God, what a player."

As for himself, McKnight pulls out a letter from the Bruins, signed by Art Ross, then the Bruins GM, advising him about the

Bruins training camp for that fall of 1951. "We are enclosing $15 for your expenses to Hershey," the letter says. "Please have this changed into American money. Please be sure you follow instructions regarding your entry permit, and bring your skates."

McKnight says that when he got to Hershey, he felt intimidated by the veteran players such as Milt Schmidt. "I'd be on the ice with Schmidt and I'd be asking myself, 'What the hell am I doing here?'" He says that he could have played for the Boston Olympics, a Bruins farm team in the Eastern Hockey League, but he decided to come home and play senior hockey. "I regret that now—that I never gave it a real shot," he says.

Later, he agreed to play in Scotland. "I had my passport and everything, but my dad had died that summer and I was needed at home." As for that Cup year, "Older men told me back then that it was something I'd never forget, and they were right. And I'm still close to Leo and Topper. But poor Chevy. That was really something."

Sooner or later, nearly everyone who knew Real Chevrefils says the same thing: "Poor Chevy."

Athletes who have fallen victim to booze or drugs—or both—include the great, the might-have-been-great and the also-rans. Among some in the last thirty years were Tim Horton, the longtime Leafs defenseman rated by Henri Richard as the strongest man in hockey, and Terry Sawchuk, the great goalie.

Sawchuk was forty and playing out the string with the New York Rangers when he died in a drunken brawl with a teammate in 1970. Horton crashed his sports car speeding from Toronto to Buffalo, for whom he was then playing, after a game in 1974. It was never proven that he was drunk, but he was a heavy drinker and on that night was primed with painkillers because of a broken jaw, so even a couple of drinks and he would have fallen asleep at the wheel.

And although he played nearly 600 NHL games, drink almost killed the Bruins center Derek Sanderson. Reggie Leach, who now counsels young players on drinking, lasted thirteen seasons and scored 61 goals for Philadelphia in 1975–76. He says he would have been an even better player if he hadn't been an alcoholic. Kevin Stevens, who scored more than 300 goals for half a dozen NHL teams, became addicted to alcohol and drugs. And then there are Bob Probert, the Red Wing and Blackhawk, and the tortured Theo Fleury, once one of the best in the game.

But most drinkers and drug takers, if they make the NHL at all, don't last long. By the time he was twenty-seven, John Kordic had already cut an anarchic path, on and off the ice, through three NHL teams over parts of six seasons. In 1991 he joined the Quebec Nordiques, where a teammate was Bryan Fogarty.

A defenseman, Fogarty was touted by some to be the next Bobby Orr. The comparison, like so many others since Orr came along, turned out to be misguided, but Fogarty had shown exceptional promise, scoring 47 goals and 155 total points for Niagara Falls in his last junior year. Still, at only twenty-two, he was as severely troubled as Kordic.

The Nordiques, praying that the two could help each other, encouraged them to live together. It didn't work. Kordic had overdosed on drugs when he died in August 1992 after a scuffle with police in a Quebec City motel. Ten years later, and seven years removed from the NHL, Fogarty died, his heart weakened by drugs and alcohol. He was thirty-two. He'd played only 156 NHL games.

Doug Harvey is another story. According to those who knew him, he was never the drinker he's been made out to be. He played more than 1,200 regular-season NHL and playoff games over nineteen seasons, fourteen of them with Montreal, where he won six Stanley Cups. He was named to ten All-Star teams; he was awarded the Norris Trophy as the league's top defenseman seven times.

Red Fisher, the Montreal sportswriter, points out that most of the players drank in those days and although Harvey may have drunk more than many of them did, it was never a problem. "He was a brilliant defenseman," Fisher says. "He owned that position until Orr came along. It was after hockey his drinking picked up because he had nothing else to do—nothing could replace hockey in his life."

Dickie Moore has praise for Harvey as a player and a person. He says that when he (Moore) joined the Canadiens the coach, Dick Irvin, was on him all the time. "I scored 33 points in 33 games that first season, but Irvin wouldn't let up, always threatening to trade me or ship me to the minors. Harvey stuck by me. He was always in my corner, teaching me, helping me. We were all better players because of him, everyone on that team."

Moore and Harvey played ten years together in Montreal. After the 1960–61 season the Canadien GM, Frank Selke—the same man who, ten years before, hadn't let Moore play for the Citadelles against Barrie—traded Harvey to the New York Rangers because he was helping to try to set up a players' union. "It broke his heart," Moore says. "I'd have a drink with him after a game and he'd say, 'Dickie, you're so lucky to be in Montreal. You don't know how bad things are in New York.' I don't think anyone knew how much it hurt him. Doug always drank, but not like the way he did after the trade. He started to drink more then."

Doug and his wife, Ursula, had four daughters and two sons. One of the sons, Glen, played Junior B in Montreal and Junior A on Prince Edward Island. He owns a pub, Buster Harveys—his nickname is Buster—on Sherbrooke Street West in Montreal. Glen is forty-four and says he was too young to have seen his father during his glory years, but that he's heard all the stories. "Ninety-nine percent of them are positive," he says. "Everybody liked my dad." On the wall by the bar, standing out from the other hockey memorabilia, is a large picture of his father. Doug and Glen Harvey share the same friendly but intense look, as well as the trademark crewcut.

Referring to the Canadiens emblem, Glen says, "Dad just bled the CH. Some people say half of him died when he was traded . . . he'd go on binges and he went through some rough times, but he ended up back doing some work for the Canadiens." Glen says that Ron Corey, then the president of the Canadiens, had made sure of that.

Sometimes, after his hockey days were over, Harvey could be seen at night, walking his dog near the old Montreal Forum at St. Catherine and Atwater. "People might shy away from him, but they shouldn't have," Moore says. "He was so proud and pleased when they recognized him and wanted to talk to him. He was very kind. He'd see a lonely-looking guy in a bar or restaurant and he'd go and talk to him, buy him a drink. He did a lot for charity, too. He helped people."

Harvey was in the Montreal General Hospital for more than a year before he died of liver failure. It was Boxing Day, 1989. He was sixty-five. "We'd hoped he'd be able to come home for Christmas with us, but the doctors wouldn't let him. So we all went to the hospital, the whole family," one of Harvey's daughters, Darlene Petsche, recalls. "It seemed to perk him up, and we got back home thinking he'd got over another hump, but then the next day we got the phone call."

She says her father had lots of visitors—old teammates and even some of the then current Canadiens. "They were terrific when Dad was in the hospital. I think that was one of the reasons he held on as long as he did. He wasn't supposed to."

But she's still angry and hurt over a story written after Harvey had taken his grandchildren to a Canadiens practice. A reporter who was there described Harvey as almost a shuffling old bum. "He wasn't at all that way," Darlene says. "That was very unfair. He was simply very sick. It was a rotten thing to write." She says her father was diagnosed as bipolar—manic depressive—a few years before he died. If the condition had been diagnosed and treated sooner, she says, perhaps he wouldn't have had his problems with alcohol. "But he was a very strong man," she says. "He managed to stop all that, the last six years or so. A lot of people don't give him credit for that."

Darlene's husband, Ted, says "I've never heard a single bad thing said about him." He remembers being on the ice with Harvey. "By then he couldn't skate, but we couldn't get the puck off him. He'd be playing with it, with this happy smile on his face. I'm very proud that he's the grandfather of my kids."

Moore saw Harvey not long before he died. "He told me, 'Dickie, if I had to do it again, I'd do the same thing.' He took everything in his stride. He never had a bad word for anybody."

Jim Morrison, the Barrie Flyer and later the Maple Leafs defenseman, admired Harvey when he played against him. Then, as their careers wound down, they played together for Quebec in the American league. "Even though I'd been in the NHL for years," Morrison says, "I could still learn from him. He was a marvel."

Morrison also visited Harvey in hospital. "He saw me coming down the hallway and he let out a holler—'Jimmy!' He was so glad to see me, and I was so glad I got there, because he was near the end. He was great."

Real Chevrefils, who led the Memorial Cup–winning Barrie Flyers, was likely as talented as Harvey but, after his promising beginning, alcohol made certain that he had a sad middle and a tragic end. "I thought he'd be the best left winger in the NHL for a good eight or ten years," Morrison says. "No one could touch him, and he proved that against Quebec. He was outstanding—skating, stickhandling, shooting. He read the play well, instinctively. That's what makes what happened to him so awful."

"I think my dad thought Chevy could do anything," says Paul Emms, Hap Emms' son. "He could literally dance on his skates and he could score and he wasn't afraid of anything. Dad had a lot of good hockey players, but Chevy was special. He played for him for three years. He still had another year of junior eligibility when he went to Hershey. I know Dad would have kept him if he didn't think he was ready." Chevrefils scored 20 goals and 48 points in 34 games for Hershey that year. "And I never saw him drink. That doesn't mean he wasn't drinking then, but I never saw it. I have no idea what caused it. He loved hockey so much."

Bill Hagan, one of Morrison's and Emms' teammates with Barrie, says it's unlikely they would have beaten Quebec without Chevrefils. "In that first game against Beliveau and the Citadelles, we were all a little apprehensive. They were supposed to kick the pants off us, and they were pretty big, too. Chevy's line started. They didn't score, but they took the play right to them, and it gave us such a lift. It seemed to set the tone for the series. I thought he was magnificent."

Sam Cancilla, the twelve-year-old back in 1951, would see Chevrefils in games and at practice. He says it would be like watching Wayne Gretzky in his prime. "The things he could do with the puck."

Hap Emms used to say that Chevrefils was the best player he ever coached. And later, in 1955, Lynn Patrick, who had succeeded Art Ross as Bruins GM, predicted that Chevrefils "will be an all-star within three years, and within five years he'll be one of the best left wings ever to play in the league." (Nearly forty years later, Lynn's son Craig, a former NHL player and longtime executive with the Rangers and the Penguins, said—in what would turn out to be a grim irony—almost the same thing about Bryan Fogarty.)

Chevrefils began to fall apart just about when he should have been at the top of his game. In fact, he played only one full, injury-free NHL season—1956–57, when he scored 31 goals over the 70-game schedule and was named to the Second All-Star Team. In 74 games over the two incomplete seasons that followed, he scored just 10 goals, and before his twenty-seventh birthday he was out of the NHL. By that time he'd scored only 104 goals in 387 regular-season games spread over parts of eight seasons, and just 5 more in 30 playoff games. This is pathetically ordinary scoring from someone who'd once been the second-best junior in Canada.

Leo Labine, who, of course, had been on that Memorial Cup team with Chevrefils, played with him in Boston. "He never seemed to have to think on the ice; it was just instinctive," Labine says. "So, seeing that much talent going down the drain was a goddamn shame. He'd be hung over in the dressing room, complaining about a headache, and I'd say, 'Chevy, you got to have a brain to have a headache.' But what are you going to do? He's one of your best players, you upset him he's not going to stop drinking. He's just going to find more things wrong with him—his groin, his stomach. He never listened to you, he never did."

This was long before most sports had any provision to help athletes with liquor or drug problems, though Lynn Patrick would have Chevrefils stay with him in Boston from time to time. But Chevrefils, according to Labine, would find a way to sneak out and go drinking.

Chevrefils, one of eight children, was born in Timmins, where his father worked in the mines. Lou Bendo, who comes from Timmins and grew up with Chevrefils, owns a prosperous real estate and insurance agency in Windsor, where he's lived for years. He was captain of Chevrefils's last team, the Windsor Bulldogs, when it won the Allan Cup in 1963. Sitting in his office on an early-spring afternoon, he talks about Chevrefils with two other hockey men who knew him well—Danny Belisle and Jack

Costello. "I was in Grade 9 with Chevy," Bendo says. "He lasted until about March or April. I remember he had an argument with a vocational teacher and smacked him and walked out. I can't remember what the argument was over, but Chevy never came back, and there was no one to make him. The next year, he went to play for Barrie. He was sixteen going on seventeen."

Belisle comes from South Porcupine, next door to Timmins. He coached the Washington Capitals in the late 1970s and now scouts for Detroit. He played in the minors with Chevrefils. "When you went to play junior in our day they set you up in a boarding house. They gave you a little guidance and direction if you wanted to go to school, but for the most part you were on your own. The first year I went to play in Guelph, I went to school. It was hard, hockey and school. The next year I didn't go to school."

Jack Costello comes from South Porcupine, too. One of his brothers was the late Les Costello—Father Les, the man behind the Flying Fathers, the team of hockey-playing priests. Les played briefly with the Leafs before getting the call to the priesthood. Another brother, Murray, a former president of the Canadian Hockey Association, played three seasons in the NHL. Jack Costello was also a good hockey player. He was on that Windsor Bulldogs team with Bendo and Chevrefils. He's a retired high school teacher. "Even if he never finished grade 9, Chevy was smart," Costello says. "We were picking up guys for the Bulldogs whose [hockey] scholarships had run out at the University of Michigan. On a road trip one time they brought along a dictionary to play a word game. You drew a word, then you had to define it. Chevy was very good. He held up his end with the university kids. He surprised a lot of people. Underneath all that crap I guess there was a real intellect. When he'd do his reading I don't know, but he had a good vocabulary."

In 1955, Boston traded Chevrefils to Detroit for Terry Sawchuk, the great goalie, who had his own demons. Jack Adams was the Detroit GM. "He tried to get Chevy to go to AA [Alcoholics Anonymous]," Danny Belisle says. "The story is that on his way to a meeting Chevy wanted to stop for a six-pack. Someone said that showed progress—before AA it would have been a case of twenty-four."

There are also reports that Adams put private detectives on him to try to keep him dry, but before long Chevrefils had turned on the charm and had them drinking with him. "Some of the drinking stories might have been funny, if the whole thing wasn't so sad," Belisle says.

Adams couldn't take it, and traded him back to Boston in January of '56. Through it all, Chevrefils never, apparently, tried to explain away or justify his drinking. About all he would say was, "When I played in Barrie I never drank a drop, honest to God. But when I went to Hershey, all the guys used to go out drinking after practice so I'd go with them. A beer here, a beer there, and I just kept going. That's it."

Lou Bendo tells much the same story. "All through junior hockey he was dedicated," Bendo says. "He never drank or ran around, but when he went to Hershey from Barrie he weighed about a 170. They wanted him to bulk up, so they suggested a couple of beers with supper. Chevy always called me 'Bubba-Louie.' He'd say, laughing, 'Hey, Bubba-Louie, I had that first beer and it was so good I kept right on going. I just couldn't stop at a couple.'"

Bendo goes on: "He'd talk in rhymes. He'd say to a bartender, 'Snap me a can, Dan,' or if someone came into the bar, 'Sit down, Jimmy Brown, and pick up a round.' Another one was when he was opening a beer: 'Watch your eye, Sy.'" Belisle says that when Chevy would drop in for a visit he'd ask, "You got a cold beer? No? How about a warm one, then?"

"Everybody was his friend, even on the ice," Bendo says. "He'd talk to the other players. You'd be threatening to punch someone out, and Chevy'd be asking him about his wife and kids. The year Barrie beat Quebec in the Memorial Cup playoffs, Beliveau fired the puck so hard it went right through the net. The officials didn't see it and the Citadelles were mad as hell, yelling and cursing. Chevy tells me, 'I skated right up to him, Bubba-Louie, and I said, "Hey, big Jean, don't shoot so hard next time."' He was funny, easygoing, at least the side we saw."

Bendo says the only thing he knows that ever seemed to bother Chevrefils was flying. "He hated it. One time I was sitting beside him on a plane and his eyes are closed and he's gripping the arms of his seat as tightly as he can. After a minute he opens his eyes and looks out and says, 'God, those people down there look small.' I said, 'Chevy, we haven't taken off yet.'"

Jack Costello was with him on a hockey tour of Europe. "In those days transatlantic flights put down in Gander, Newfoundland," Costello says. "It's really foggy and we can't see a thing and *bang*, we hit the runway—hit it really hard. It scared the hell out of everyone. Chevy's really shaken up. He's the first one off the plane, and he's running through the airport, and there's got to be at least nine or ten turns—down one corridor, up another—and I'm following him and finally we come right out at the bar. I asked him how the hell he knew the way, and he said that some years back he'd gone overseas with the Rangers and the Bruins for an exhibition series, and he'd remembered from back then where it was. He used to call me 'Johnny.' I can still see him, sitting there at that bar, raising a beer in his huge hand and saying, 'Well, Johnny, here's to across the ocean.'"

Danny Belisle says, "I never heard him poor-mouth anyone. He never said, 'Jesus, they screwed me.' Athletes had a tendency, at least in those days, if they were traded or benched or sent down or whatever, to blame everyone but themselves—the coach, the GM, the owner. Chevy was never like that."

Costello says, "A lot of people tried to help him, but he liked what he was doing. He knew the consequences were death and I think he chose to go that way."

Chevrefils was married when he was young to a girl he'd grown up with in Timmins, Claudette Roy. Friends say that she eventually drank, too. "I guess she tried to keep up with him," one said. "She certainly didn't start out as a drinker." Bendo remembers her from high school. "She was so beautiful and sweet and quiet."

Belisle says that when they were playing together for the Los Angeles Blades, the team owners flew Claudette out to look after Real. It was disastrous. They fought and drank out there and she had to go back home.

One of Chevrefils's brothers, Maurice, lives outside Hull, across the Ottawa River from Ottawa. He was a hockey player, too, with the Johnstown Jets in the old International Hockey League and then in senior hockey in Kapuskasing. He was a couple of years younger than Real. When he was a youngster, Hap Emms had brought him to Barrie to play Junior B. "Emms wanted Real, and the Citadelles were after him, too. They told him that if he came to Quebec they'd have a spot for me, too," Maurice says. "So Hap said, 'Well, if that's the case, we'll bring you to Barrie and you can play here.' That's how much he wanted Real."

But Maurice says he was too close to his brother to realize how good he was. "A while ago I was in a store in Ottawa and I picked up a hockey book. It quoted Lynn Patrick as saying what a great player he might have been and then about the booze getting to him. I don't know what happened. Real never told me. We never talked about it." He says he didn't know his brother's wife well. "I never even had a meal at their house," he says. "When we'd meet, it'd be at our dad's."

Ron Keast played Junior B with another one of Chevrefils's brothers. He says that even when it looked as if he'd be an NHL star, Real remained open and friendly; it never went to his head.

"He'd come back to Timmins and work for Doran's Brewery and you'd see him around town, delivering beer to the taverns, and he always had a big smile and hello. I guess, looking back, working for a brewery was a pretty good job for Chevy, but we didn't know about his drinking then."

Jim Jackson, who knew Chevrefils well back then and caddied for him at golf tournaments in Northern Ontario, says that if it hadn't been for hockey, and alcohol, Chevrefils could have made a career in golf. On a summer's day, Jackson and a few other friends of Chevrefils are in the coffee shop at the McIntyre Arena in Timmins.

The arena is on the old McIntyre mining property. It opened in 1938 and was inaugurated by the Maple Leafs with an intra-squad game. It is one of the classic old arenas in Ontario, and the coffee shop's walls are covered with photographs of hockey players from the Timmins area who skated there, including Dean Prentice, twenty years in the NHL, largely with the Rangers; Walter Tkachuk, also a Ranger and one of the NHL's best centers in the sixties and the seventies; Pete Babando, whose goal for Detroit in the second overtime period of the seventh game of the 1950 Stanley Cup final sank the Rangers, 4–3. The Mahovliches are there, too, and Bob Nevin—eighteen NHL years, mostly with the Leafs and Rangers. And, of course, Chevrefils.

Jackson says that, as with a lot of things, Chevrefils didn't take his golf seriously. "But people around Chevy sure did. When he got to the first tee the clubhouse would empty, everyone coming out to watch him hit, but you had to be quick because he'd tee it up, not waste a second, and *bang*, it'd be gone, long and straight. He didn't fool around."

Another friend of Chevrefils interrupts. He mentions Sergio Garcia, one of the best golfers in the world. At one time Garcia had a seemingly interminable routine while he stood over the ball of flexing and unflexing his fingers around his club before he would swing. "Hell, Chevy could drink a beer in the time Sergio takes to do his waggle," the man says.

Jackson continues, describing Chevrefils's golf game. "One time he hits off at a short par four, 330 yards, something like that—just tees it up and *bang*, away it goes. We lost it in the sun or something. We walked right straight up to the green because he always hit them dead straight, but no ball anywhere. Someone says look in the cup.

"Well, if you figure that's the story, that it's there in the cup, a hole-in-one on a par four, you're wrong. When we do find it, it's about fifteen yards over the green, up against a fence. That means Chevy must have hit that ball about 350 yards. And remember, back then there were no juiced-up balls and titanium-shaft, big-headed clubs. He was so strong. He had hands like shovels. We'd go into tournaments and he'd be great for the first couple of days, then he'd get into the booze and that'd be it."

"And he had a temper, too, sometimes, when he'd been drinking," another friend says. "I remember him knocking a guy right out his chair without even getting up."

Real and Claudette separated in 1962, and Claudette eventually returned to Timmins with their six children. Real stayed in Windsor. A son died in 1976 of hepatitis. His funeral was likely the last time Chevrefils went home to Timmins. One of his daughters, Denise, who was just a child when her parents separated, says that she saw her father only three times after the move back—"at his dad's funeral, at his mother's funeral and at my brother's funeral."

In spite of the turbulent marriage, friends said the separation seemed to make Chevrefils drink even more. When he qualified for his NHL pension it was worth about $130 a month. Jimmy Skinner, the Red Wings executive, arranged for him to get another $200 from a special NHL fund for needy ex-players. By this time Lou Bendo owned the Windsor Arena and he arranged for Chevrefils to pick up his money—not all at once—from the arena manager, Siro Martinello. (Martinello has since died.) He had to be presentable before Martinello would give him a nickel. Alan Halberstadt wrote in the *Windsor Star* that

"Chevy is there every Monday morning at 11 o'clock, a black tie with a knot the size of a chestnut, starched white shirt, black and yellow dress sweater with a faded Boston Bruins crest located, aptly, near his heart."

According to Halberstadt, only once did Martinello have to send Chevrefils home empty-handed because he'd broken the dress code and arrived looking slovenly. "Chevy's a very nice person," Martinello told Halberstadt. "That's why I try to get him to straighten out." But Halberstadt quotes Lynn Patrick as saying that Chevrefils and Claudette "used to fight like cats and dogs. A couple of times he came to practice scratched like he'd run through a rosebush."

Janice Banigan worked at Windsor's Downtown Mission. Chevrefils was often there. "I didn't know then who he was, that he was once a hockey star," she says. "I do remember wondering if we could have done something for him, but I'm not sure we could have. I think by that point he'd decided to drink himself to death. I don't remember much else. All he'd have was a cup of coffee. He'd sit by himself in the corner and have his coffee and leave. He was always well behaved, always polite."

In a piece in the *Toronto Star* in 1998, Banigan wrote about Chevrefils going off to shovel snow with other men from the mission on a bitterly cold day for less than a dollar an hour. "Real had only one glove, with two fingers missing. When he returned his hands were fiery red . . . He had no boots, either, only worn old shoes." She said she'd asked him about his clothes and all he'd said was, "Don't worry. I'll be okay."

Even now, she says, memories of the man who turned out to be Real Chevrefils are vivid, or as vivid as they can be of a man who gave away so little of himself. "About all he ever said to me was that he was okay, and thanks, that's all. But I can still see and hear him. I tried to put the pieces together after he died, but it was hard. Most of the people who came to the mission wanted something, or needed something. The alcoholics wanted money for liquor, the hungry naturally wanted food. If someone doesn't want something, it flags them, they stand out. I suppose that's why I remembered him. He never made demands, never asked for much more than coffee. He hardly said anything. He looked unwell—thin, and thinning hair—but when someone doesn't look into your eyes and you can't see into his, what do you know about him? It was only after he died and I saw a picture of him I realized he was the man whom I'd see at the mission."

However, in spite of his seeming indifference to his condition or his past, at least one friend says Chevrefils showed occasional flashes of pride. For example, while sick or drying out at Windsor's Hôtel-Dieu Hospital, he would tell nurses that he hadn't always been a wreck like this, that he'd once scored 30 goals for the Boston Bruins.

When he wasn't at the mission or in the hospital, Chevrefils would likely be with his older brother Roly, who is dead now, too, at the Lincoln or St. Clair taverns, which are now long gone. More than once he tried to rationalize his life to friends. "Peace of mind, that's all I ever asked the Lord for, and that's what I've got."

He died in January 1981, at the Hôtel-Dieu. He was forty-eight. According to the *Windsor Star*, the doctor who attended him declined to release the cause of death. It quotes him as saying that anyone who knew Chevrefils's background would know what killed him.

At his funeral, six former teammates from the Windsor Bulldogs, including Lou Bendo and Jack Costello, were pall-bearers. But there wasn't much of a turnout. Among the forty or so other people there, besides relatives, were the longtime Bruins player, coach and executive Milt Schmidt, and Jimmy Skinner, and Marc Reaume, the former Leaf and Red Wing. Chevrefils was buried at Heavenly Rest Cemetery on the outskirts of Windsor.

A small stone, lying flat, marks his grave. On this cold, early April day, it is streaked with snow. Suddenly, a gust of wind whips the snow away, baring the inscription. It reads: "Chevy, number 12, May 2, 1932–Jan. 8, 1981." On an upper corner is the Boston Bruins emblem.

Hockey on the Rez

THE PAS, MANITOBA • Glen Watson is a driven man. He's friendly, but he's also tense and restless. Hockey is his life. Right now the season is just underway, so he's anxious to see whether the team he put together over the summer has what it takes. "He's got a temper, so you don't want to be on his bad side," Jon Romic, one of his players, says. "When we practice, we practice hard. There's no fooling around. He's okay, though, he's good to play for."

Watson is the coach and general manager of the Opaskwayak Cree Nation (OCN) Blizzard, a Native-owned team in the Manitoba Junior Hockey League. He's forty, built like a hockey player in his prime, and is missing a couple of front teeth, which seems about right, too. He's in his office at the rink. He's wearing a nylon tracksuit, sweating a bit; a towel is wrapped around his neck. It's only eight o'clock in the morning, but he has already had a half-hour workout on a stationary bike before morning practice. "I love coming to the rink, working with the kids, teaching them," he says. "I love the routine. I could never walk away from it."

Watson's two older brothers, Joe and Jim, had solid careers with the Philadelphia Flyers. Glen didn't make it that far. He played three years for the Red Deer Rustlers of the Alberta Junior Hockey League, and he was trying out for Winston-Salem in the East Coast Hockey League when he blew out his knee. After playing senior hockey in British Columbia, he had stops in South Africa and Britain. He came home and became assistant coach of the Quesnel, B.C., juniors in the Rocky Mountain league, taking over as coach halfway through the season when the team was struggling. Next came four years at Estevan in the Saskatchewan Junior Hockey League—a sister league to the MJHL—and then two in Prince George, in the BCJHL.

He has just signed his second two-year contract with the OCN Blizzard. The team has been going for seven years and has been league champions the last four. Six of the players are from the First Nations, two of these from the Opaskwayak reserve. But, according to Louis Personius, an OCN director, although the reserve owns the team, it wants the best players it can get on the ice, regardless of race. "We don't care if they're twenty Cree or twenty white," he says.

And Watson says, "One of the reasons we keep winning is that we do extensive recruiting. We have kids from Ontario, Quebec . . . We got one from Philadelphia, another from Minnesota. The Philly kid has been here three years. He has fit right in."

Pulling the lid off a Tim Hortons coffee and trying to relax, he says, "Some kids come out of junior and think they know it all, but they don't—some don't have a goddamn clue. But you can't teach them because, like I said, they think they know every-thing. And I'm not interested in a kid, no matter how much tal-ent he has, if he just wants to piss around—they're just wasting my time and their own. I want a solid work ethic. Some kids can't be coached; I don't need them. I want kids with grit who want to learn, because if I've learned anything from hockey it's that you never stop learning. There's always someone who has something to teach you."

This year, Watson points out, the league has taken out the red line, except for icing. "It really opens the game up," he says. "It gives you a better chance to see what a kid can do. There's less obstruction. But everything is changing in hockey. The kids are getting so big. I look at my brothers' sweaters when they played for the Flyers. My kids couldn't get into them. That's how big they're getting. They gotta widen the rinks, give them more space."

Jon Romic, from Oakville, Ontario, just west of Toronto, the player who says you don't want to be on Coach Watson's bad side, is an earnest and purposeful young man. He is eighteen and, in spite of his size—six feet two inches and more than 200 pounds—he still looks young. At present, hockey is his whole life. He says that Watson spotted him at a hockey camp last summer and asked him right away whether he'd be interested in playing in The Pas.

"I made a decision to put hockey first, so I came right up," he says. "I came up blind. I knew nothing about it. I love it up here; I really do. I'm not just saying it. I'm on the ice every day, and then when you skate out for a game and hear those cheers, it's a great feeling. I have a wonderful billet, too. They've taken me in, just like family. I couldn't ask for anything better."

Romic tells me he got a late start—he was ten before he skated—but he has made up for it through hard work. "I sacrificed a lot," he says. "I didn't go out with my friends. All I did in summers was skate and work out. When I was younger, a lot of guys said I wouldn't make it because I was so far behind. But here I am—and most of them have quit."

And he hasn't forgotten a coach who made a lot of it happen. "His name is Rick Crumpton and he coached me in pee-wee," Romic says. "Until he saw me I was just playing house league. He gave me my first break, putting me on a rep team. I'll never forget that. Every player brings his own dimension. I guess one of the most important characteristics is discipline, on and off the ice. That's what I try to achieve."

Outside, it's a glorious fall day. Inside, the players are filing into their dressing room to get ready for their morning skate. A few of them have five o'clock shadows. Others, no matter how big they are, still look like Romic: fresh-faced youngsters, even with those wispy beards under the lower lip—some have standard goatees—that every fashionable hockey player between fifteen and twenty-five seems to sport. Today is Friday, and the Blizzard play tonight, tomorrow night and Sunday afternoon—three games in three days. So much for junior hockey in the north.

Watson says what others might consider isolation doesn't bother him. He comes from Smithers, in northern B.C., a dot on the map, "I like small towns," he says, so for the time being, anyway, he's content. "I mean, if I wanted to move up to the Western Hockey League, I'd have to start at thirteen or fifteen thousand as an assistant coach, and you can't survive on that. At my level I enjoy what I do, trying to guide the kids. If the opportunity came up I'd look at it, but I'm not going banging on any doors—I'm tired of that bullshit. There's a lot of politics in the Western Hockey League. If you played in the league you stand a good chance of getting a job whether you deserve one or not. It's the buddy system. Maybe down the road I'll look at pro teams in the States. In hockey, you meet a lot of people in the community, and there are college scouts and pro scouts. I like that. Hockey is a big network, but a lot of people know who I am. That's another thing—being a pro scout. I think I'd like that."

The Pas is a six-hour drive north of Winnipeg—and for five of those hours there isn't much to look at but trees and bush. And it's by road that most people make the trip—the twice-a-week train takes longer. It runs through to Churchill and it's pretty busy in the summer with tourists off to see the polar bears and off to Hudson Bay for the Beluga whales. Things are much quieter in winter. Flights, meanwhile, depending on bookings, can cost anywhere from $200 to more than $800.

Approaching The Pas early on a warm, overcast autumn morning, the flat gray-white northern sky is riven by flocks of Canada geese flying high in their ragged vees. The main road, Manitoba Highway 6, is lined by rocks, slim white birches with yellow leaves, and small evergreens. Through the trees, deer can be seen now and then, wide-eyed, slim and elegant as fashion models. At one point two large moose, rough looking in their thick coats, which seem uncharacteristically dark, amble across the road, confident and unmindful of the car.

Otherwise it is still—not a breath of wind. It's as if one were caught in a photograph or a painting. The area is rich in colorfully Canadian names. Besides The Pas, Flin Flon is about ninety minutes northwest. A bit nearer is Cranberry Portage.

And there is Snow Lake, Loonhead Lake and Goose Lake, Cormorant and Grass River, Pukatawagan and Payuk.

The original Cree name for The Pas means "where the river narrows." The river is the Saskatchewan. The first European settlers came to the area when the Hudson's Bay Company opened a fur trading post at nearby Cumberland House in the late eighteenth century. Then came mining, agriculture and forestry. Fire almost destroyed the town in 1913, and Spanish flu, the scourge of Europe and North America after the First World War, killed hundreds in 1919. According to reports at the time, "streets were deserted and volunteers went from house to house to maintain firewood in the homes of the sick and dying."

By the early 1900s the railway was humming, but although the first automobile, nicknamed "The Buzzwagon," arrived in 1919, the highway to Winnipeg wasn't opened until 1939.

In all, there are about 13,000 people in the region. The Pas proper has about 6,000, most of them white; the Rural Municipality of Kelsey—the farming area around The Pas—has a couple of thousand more. And across the Saskatchewan River from town, the Opaskwayak Cree Nation (OCN), is home to more than 4,000 First Nations people.

The rink, the Gordon Lathlin Memorial Centre, is named for a Cree chief. It's on the Cree side of the river and is owned by the Cree Nation. It can hold up to 1,300 people if they're jammed in, and they have been. It's about twenty years old, a bit rickety, and there's already talk of raising money for a new one. But $250,000 was spent recently to upgrade the dressing rooms, which are as spacious and well outfitted as many semi-pro dressing rooms. Every game is videotaped, and coaches and players review them in a new lounge on a thirty-six-inch TV set. There's also a workout area. And for fans who want a regular dose of OCN hockey news, the team has its own Web site.

Next door to the arena is the kind of shopping mall that might be found in suburban Lethbridge, London or Saint John. It's busy with kids, many of them aboriginal and most of them in the baggy dress favored by the young everywhere. Next door to the mall is a swank new hotel, the Kikiwak Inn. Grey Goose Bus Line coaches regularly bring visitors from Winnipeg. Many of them are in their seventies and eighties, and even those on walkers, after checking into the Kikiwak, board the bus again to be driven to the glittering casino a couple of minutes away, where the first five bucks' worth of chips is on the house.

There's also a new high school on the reservation and a housing subdivision. All were built with money from a land claim settlement with the federal government and are operated by the Cree.

On the banks of the Saskatchewan River, a few hundred yards from the arena, a middle-aged Native man is camping out. He has a pup tent and a couple of lawn chairs, and he has built a small firepit. He's on his own; no one appears to be paying him any mind. He says his name is Samuel Roderick MacGillvary and that he is protesting against housing conditions for Native Canadians. This is his fifty-eighth day here, he says, following two months on the other side of the river—the south side, The Pas side.

Measuring his words, he speaks softly, seemingly without anger. He says that living conditions off the reserve are as tough as ever. For example, forty-four people have to share a three-bedroom house in Lynn Lake, up north, and thirty-two children live in one house at Moose Lake, a little to the east. He has copies of a letter he wrote to Prime Minister Jean Chrétien, but he has not had a reply. He says he's prepared to stay on the riverbank for "four winters, four springs, four summers and four falls." Today is fall and it's lovely, but winter isn't far away.

Across the river from him, The Pas looks like any western small town: wide main streets, three or four hotels and motels and taverns, government offices, a couple of video shops and fast-food outlets and restaurants. St. Anthony's Hospital—one of the few buildings over three stories—is as big and imposing as any big-city building but, just as in many Canadian communities, some if its wards have been shut down. There's a good-sized library and a museum. On this particular morning a dusty red pickup truck is parked near the post office; a sticker on is rear window reads, "God Bless Canada."

Whites and First Nations people say the hockey team's success has helped to improve relations between their two communities. They've been ugly in the recent past. Not that long ago, movie theaters in The Pas were segregated, and the Cree even had a hard time being served in stores there.

And just more than thirty years ago, three white men raped and murdered Helen Betty Osborne, a Native teenager they'd pulled into their car as she walked home from school, prompting one of the worst periods for race relations in Canadian history—just as bad as the situation forty years ago in Mississippi, when three civil rights workers, including a young black man, were lynched. Betty Osborne's murderers weren't brought to trial for ten years.

But even with the advent of the Blizzard, there have been tragedies. John Stackhouse, in one of a series of articles in *The Globe and Mail* in 2001, wrote about Perry Young. He was a local Cree hockey star who experienced intense pressure to make the team. When things didn't work out, he killed himself. Young's family is still angry and bitter. His mother told Stackhouse that hockey's highly competitive white system ignores many of the problems Native youngsters must face. She says that the OCN Blizzard, with its drive for success on the ice, is at least partly responsible for her son's death.

The close-knit Tootoo brothers, Terence and Jordin (Jordin, the younger of the two, is the first Inuit player to play in the NHL), both played for the Blizzard. Terence was twenty-two in August 2002 and had just signed a contract with Roanoke of the ECHL when shortly after being charged with drunken driving, he committed suicide with a shotgun near Brandon, Manitoba. Once again, disappointment in hockey—in this case that he wasn't going to the NHL—may have led to the suicide.

Pat Personius, at sixty-six the Cree elder on the OCN board, agrees that life for Native youngsters is especially tough. "The thing is with our kids, the hockey players, they get with their friends and they can't keep the curfew, they got no respect," he says. "Sure, there's a lot of pressure and sometimes, I guess, they can't handle it. But if parents have a kid that's playing hockey, they have to make sure they keep the curfew, look after themselves. Kids start fooling around, and soon you got nothing. But the Tootoos were good, they were special."

He says that the team's success has put the Opaskwayak Cree Nation on the map. "We have no problems getting coaches or players because we're such a good organization. We had more than 150 kids from all over at our training camp. Most teams get about fifty. They were in hotels, motels, campers . . . "

Personius estimates that it costs about $400,000 a year to run the Blizzard—salaries, travel, equipment, insurance, what have you. On a three-game weekend on the road, it can be a trip of more than 700 kilometers just to get to the first game.

Louis Personius, Pat's younger brother, says, "Before the hockey there was little or no communication between the white and the Native people, but there is now. There's no doubt about that. Whites in the town and from the mill, too, they all say that."

Pat goes on, "The hockey players are nice kids. And they're good role models for our kids on the reserve, especially the Tootoos." He turns to Louis. "Hey, maybe we should go down to Nashville and see him." Then he says proudly, "Y'know, the other night he was on TV being interviewed and he was wearing his Blizzard jersey."

Pat and Louis have a ninety-four-year-old uncle. "He's slowing down," Lou says, "but he loves hockey. He'd stay in an arena all day. Heck, if it's a tournament, he'd probably sleep there."

The Personius brothers went to Halifax last year, where the Blizzard narrowly lost in the Royal Bank Cup final for the Canadian Junior A championship. Louis drove down. "It took four-and-a-half days," he says. Pat went by air.

Right now, Pat is excited about a goalie who's just arrived from Quebec. He was at the St. Louis Blues camp. "You should see him," Pat says. "He's big—gotta be about seven feet in his skates."

After the Friday-morning skate, Watson and four players head off for the weekly live hit on CJAR radio. The radio reporter,

Kris Menard, who is also the technician, is setting up his equipment in the corner of the local A&W under black-and-white photographs that celebrate The Pas's fur trappers' festival. Menard, in a beard and an Oakland A's baseball cap, is big and broad enough to be an offensive lineman with the Winnipeg Blue Bombers. He is only twenty-one, but he says he has been in broadcasting in Thompson and The Pas since he was sixteen.

Watson wants his players to be either working or going to school. Five or six are in high school and a few more are at a community college. As Watson sits down near the mike and Menard checks his sound levels, he gives one of the players hell for not showing up at a job. "I don't want you just sitting around on your ass," Watson says. "I goddamn well mean that."

The player is eighteen-year-old Paul Wallmann. He comes from Souris, in southwestern Manitoba. "I'm not gonna just sit around," he says. He says it softly and respectfully, but he has an easy smile, as if he's heard it all before.

Before anything more can be said, the broadcast begins. Watson talks about the state of the team and then various promotions, including a raffle, something called "Bowling for Turkeys" and a free skate after Sunday's afternoon game where kids may meet the players and get autographs. And there's also the upcoming visit of the Philadelphia Flyers alumni, arranged by Watson's brother Joe, who works for the Flyers. At that point Kris Menard stresses the tie between the Flyers and the north, reminding his listeners that former Flyers Bobby Clarke and Reggie Leach played for Flin Flon, an hour or so up the road. "Reggie is a good speaker," Watson says. Leach is Aboriginal, Watson says, and a good role model. "He comes up here and the kids listen to him."

Then it's the players' turn. They chip in their two bits about themselves, the thrill of playing hockey for the Blizzard and the coming games.

But there's a deep love of hockey that's been part of The Pas long before the Blizzard came about. Five or six men in their fifties and older are sitting nearby. When the broadcast wraps up, Gary Krawchuk, who grew up in Kirkland Lake, says that The Pas was starved for hockey before the Blizzard. "They'd get five or six hundred out just to watch oldtimers games against Flin Flon," he says.

Ronald Cox is from The Pas, where he worked for the Canadian National Railway. He's seventy-two, broad-shouldered, white-haired and wears glasses. He looks distinguished, for an old hockey player. "We played intermediate and senior hockey," he says. "There was the Boundary Hockey League, teams from Manitoba and Saskatchewan. Another one was the Carrot River Valley League. It was pretty good hockey." He remembers playing against Hudson Bay, Dauphin, Russell, Tisdale, Nipawin and Yorkton. "There were others, too. I can't remember them all. You should talk to Harold Wells. He coached us after he had to quit playing."

Harold Wells is seventy-five. "We had trouble getting into leagues back then because we were so far north," he says. "In those days, going to Yorkton was a long trip; not like now, when they go all over."

Wells played senior hockey for The Pas and in Flin Flon. In Flin Flon, the mining companies subsidized the team. "We worked three hours a day in the mines and they paid us for eight," he says. He had a tryout with the Victoria Cougars of the Pacific Coast Hockey League, and when that didn't work out he took a bus to Nanaimo, which had a team in a B.C. senior league. "They offered me a hundred dollars a month and said if I wanted they'd put me in a mine. They had a coal mine. But it was going to shut down, so there wasn't much future. I came back here a year or so later and played for the Huskies."

He also played in Churchill for three months when a job took him there. "That'd be 1952, I guess. It was a really good league—Canadian army, navy and air force had teams. There were a lot of people up there. The American army and air force had teams, too. We had six in all. I played for the Foundation, the construction company. That was the last time I played, because I got polio. I was twenty-four. I really missed it.

"When I got to where I could walk with a cane a bit I started to manage the senior Huskies, and then I coached them for two or three years. When I got to be thirty, I packed it in." He says that over the years, as players got older, and senior and intermediate hockey wasn't able to keep attracting younger players, the Huskies and their leagues went out of business.

More than forty years later he still follows hockey, but it's the NHL, not the Blizzard. He hasn't even been to a Blizzard game. "It's almost an entirely imported team," he says. "I don't pay much attention to them. I was hoping they'd use a lot more locals. That disappoints me. I'd like to see kids from around here."

Friday evening in the arena's lobby, fans are buying pop and hot dogs and candy while they wait for the game to begin. On the wall beside the hot dog stand are large portraits of Terence Tootoo and another Blizzard player, Cliff Duchesne. Duchesne was twenty-two when he was killed on Christmas Day, 2000. He was on a new snowmobile—he'd just bought it for himself—

and was crossing a bridge near Thompson when one of the machine's skis caught the bridge's railing. Duchesne was thrown into the Burntwood River, where he was drowned. Police called it a "tragic, freak accident." They said neither alcohol nor speed contributed to it.

Outside the Blizzard dressing room, the assistant coaches—they have regular jobs and, Watson says, are not paid much for hockey—chat with each other. Watson is pacing, trying to relax but not doing much of a job at it. He won't go into the dressing room until just before the team goes onto the ice. Then he'll announce the starting lineup and give a short pep talk. Only the trainers are in there now with the players.

Watson does loosen up a bit when another assistant coach, Jerry Mosiondz, arrives. He's an engineer at Tolko, a paper company and the region's biggest employer. He's a young-looking forty-four, short and stocky, and in his glasses could pass for a graduate student. But he played junior hockey in southern Manitoba and has been with the Blizzard from the start. He's showing off his nose. After six years he's finally got around to having it fixed. It was broken playing old-timers' hockey. The operation was two days ago and he was released yesterday from hospital.

"That's the trouble with old-timers'," he says. "Guys still trying to make their mark, swing their sticks, showing us how close they came to making the big time. Jesus. Guy hit me square in the face." He's pleased with his new nose; it looks like most noses that haven't been banged about. Mosiondz says the doctor told him he might end up with two black eyes after surgery, but there isn't a trace of even one. He says, "I said, 'Doc, I end up with a black eye, *you* end up with a black eye.'"

Because he's not very big, Mosiondz knows the value of size in today's game. "When we began, we brought in some big guys to make sure we weren't going to be pushed around, be the league's doormats. We made our point. Our penalty minutes are down but the other teams are still wary. We have a reputation for toughness."

He likes having local players on the team, but at the same time he says there's no pressure to sign a kid just because he comes from The Pas or the Cree nation. "If they're on the team it's because they earned it," he says. "We've done more to bring this community together in a few years than the politicians have ever done."

Terry Desjarlais agrees. He comes in from the dressing room. A big, amiable man in his forties, he's an assistant trainer. He's waving the shaft of a stick, its blade broken off. He's grinning, but he means business. "You better speak to Sher-Wood. They shouldn't be breaking like this," he tells Watson, referring to the hockey stick manufacturer. "This is the second one Mark's broken in two games, just taking a shot. The other was right up under the glove." Mark is Mark Wallmann, a center, one of the best players on the team and the older brother of Paul Wallmann.

Desjarlais comes from Fort Qu'Appelle, Saskatchewan, the birthplace of Eddie Shore. When he is isn't at the rink—and he usually is—he's a carpenter. He's an Aboriginal, and he came to The Pas to help his sister build a house. And he decided to stay. "Hockey is meant to be part time, but it's pretty well taken over my life," he says. "Both my sons play hockey—one Junior B here, for the OCN Storm, the other midget."

The time between seasons seems long, he says. "You gotta wait three or four months until the boys are back again. You miss them. You wonder how they're getting on. I like sitting and talking to them, finding out how their careers are going. They're dedicated, and so is the coaching staff. And we've had lots of good kids come and go. Just meeting the kids and sitting, talking to them on their days off, telling stories, and then you look at the clock and four hours is gone." One player Desjarlais remembers fondly was a Swede, Tobias Hall, who now is playing back in Sweden. "When he was here he heard someone on TV use that old line about Swedish hockey players going into the corner with a dozen eggs in their pockets and not breaking one," he says. "He told me that made him really mad. He turned out to be one of our toughest players.

"And I'll tell you another thing, this hockey team is the best thing that has happened to the north in years. Before this team, the river was a real social, as well as geographic, dividing line between the town and the reserve. Now everybody talks hockey."

Aaron Starr and Everett Bear, nice-looking and polite, are two of the First Nations players with the Blizzard. Starr, a center, is the team's leading scorer early in the season. He is from Saskatoon. He played his minor hockey in Saskatchewan, and he spent a year with the Saskatoon Blades of the WHL. He came up to The Pas after touring Finland with a team of Native players coached by Ted Nolan, the former Buffalo Sabres coach, who comes from a reserve outside Sault Ste. Marie, Ontario. Two other players on that team had played in The Pas—Darcy Johnson, who has gone on to play professionally in the United States, and Terence Tootoo. "They were a lot older than me, but they said what a great place The Pas was, and it is," Starr says. "It's the best place I've ever played." At twenty, this is his last year in junior. Next year he hopes to go to the University of Manitoba or the University of New Brunswick.

Starr says he still occasionally hears racist remarks from some fans, but not from opposing players. For the most part, he says, racism seems a thing of the past, at least as far as junior hockey goes.

"Saskatchewan used to be bad, people yelling stuff at us. I played in Kindersley one year, and last year we went to Humboldt and it was bad, yeah. They'd yell out racial slurs. And one time in Kindersley they threw cans of Lysol on the ice, meaning that we were dirty. But in our league now, it's not a problem. I heard it was a lot worse for OCN when the team started a few years ago—in Estevan, and stories about Dauphin, [people] leaving pamphlets on the bus, stuff like that. But it's okay now."

Bear agrees. "I really don't think racism is what it used to be," he says.

One of the locals on the team is Donald Melnyk, from the Opaskwayak reserve. He says he still hears the rare racist taunt and it makes him mad, "but I try not to let it get me down, and I guess it's not like it used to be."

Bear, Starr and Melnyk all feel that playing in The Pas is, in Bear's words, "awesome. The fans are amazing." OCN, Bear says, is the only team that went after him seriously when he was about to graduate from midget. "Other teams sent me stuff, and I went to a camp in Brandon when I was fifteen, but OCN phoned my house and actually came there and showed they were interested in me," he says. Watson, he says, is the best coach he's ever had. "He likes tough, physical play and defense. Sorta my game."

Bear comes from a reserve ten minutes from Whitewood, in southeastern Saskatchewan. "It was a good place to grow up. That's where I got into hockey." He says Whitewood is "a really small place. The Pas is a lot bigger." Like Starr, he's in his final year with the team. He hopes to go to university in the States.

Melnyk says he'd like to play professionally, perhaps in the East Coast league. He's just turning eighteen, and this is his second year with the Blizzard. He say he's not aware of any pressure being put on him because he's from The Pas. "I just try to play my game and not think about it," he says. "Play hard and have fun."

About six hundred people, Natives and white, are in the arena tonight to see the Blizzard play the Winnipeg Blues. "The crowds have dropped a bit—I guess because we're always winning," coach and GM Watson says. "But it's early in the season. They'll get back to eight or nine hundred." When "O Canada" is played, most of the crowd joins in the singing and all the men, young and old, remove their hats. The second the singing stops, the cheering for the Blizzard starts.

Watson is right about the lack of a red line opening up the game, and the OCN Blizzard, a fast-skating team, takes advantage of it. Winnipeg's coach, Billy Keane, the brother of NHL veteran Mike Keane, says he always hopes his team can feed off the noisy, partisan crowds in The Pas. "There's a ton of energy in that rink. It works for some of our guys. Some of the younger ones end up gawking around." There isn't much gawking tonight, although the Blizzard rallies in the third period to win 6–3. As the game winds down there's a series of brawls.

Greg Hunter is one of the Blizzard's assistant coaches. He's from Cambridge, near Kitchener, Ontario. He teaches phys ed at the local high school. He's thirty-seven and is built like a defenseman, although he played center. "I liked the bump and grind of hockey." A crooked scar runs well up his cheek from the right-hand corner of his mouth.

He was playing his first year for the Dixie Beehives, a Tier II Junior A team from just west of Toronto. He jumped over the boards to get into the play, and an opponent's flying skate cut him. "We didn't wear face guards then, and I could tell right away something was wrong," he says. "For one thing, my mouthpiece was in about three pieces on the ice—" He pauses, then says, "This is a funny story," and continues: "Our trainer jumped on the ice. He was a butcher—and you'd think he'd be used to the sight of blood. It was squirting all over and he put a towel on it and then he fainted—fainted right there. Our captain caught him, took him to the bench and then came back for me.

"My jaw was broken. I lost six teeth and took about seventy-five stitches. It was too bad, but my mother was at the game. I mean, they're looking at my teeth through my cheek. I was out six weeks. I came back with my jaw wired shut and wearing a cage. It was a fluke thing. His skates came right up in the air, about six feet."

Hunter, like any hockey player, sooner or later had to make a decision about his future. "I had a good year, but when I came back for my second I noticed guys with skills slightly higher than mine. Not that much higher, but higher. It was heartbreaking at the time to realize that you aren't going to get there, but everything has worked out for the best."

He left Ontario for Acadia University in Wolfville, Nova Scotia, for a degree in education. In his last year he helped out with midget coaching and decided he still wanted to be part of hockey. There were stops back in Ontario and then at Notre Dame, the renowned high school and hockey power in Wilcox, Saskatchewan. There he met the woman he was to marry. She came from The Pas, so they moved here. "It was a perfect time for me because the Blizzard was just being formed," Hunter says.

One of his most distinct memories is that of seeing Jordin and Terence Tootoo for the first time. "We were having tryouts in Thompson and I guess they were thirteen and fifteen. They had all the passion for the game you just pray your players will have. I gave them our card, told them about the Blizzard if they ever wanted to play junior. Then, being a southern guy, used to teams and leagues, I asked them who they played against in Rankin Inlet. They just grinned and pointed at each other. That's who they played against, each other."

Hunter says he still gets upset when he thinks about Terence Tootoo's death. "I'd just been at a hockey school with him," he says. "He'd told me how much he was looking forward to going back to Roanoke. You know he was assistant captain there his first year? He was a wonderful guy."

That evening, before the second game, it's even warmer than yesterday. It's like summer. A couple of hundred fans mill around outside the arena smoking. The arena, apart presumably from St. Anthony's Hospital, appears to be about the only place in The Pas where smoking isn't allowed. Although Manitoba is proposing strict legislation that would ban smoking just about everywhere, indoors and out, it isn't law, yet. No alcohol is served at the arena, either.

Back inside, the Blizzard coaches are unnaturally quiet. No more cracks about Jerry Mosiondz's nose. It turns out that one of the maintenance workers, a thirty-eight-year-old former hockey player named Brian Dorian, was killed after last night's game when he fell down the stairs at the arena. No one saw him fall, but he was dead when his body was found. There was some talk of postponing the game, but it was decided to go ahead with it. There'll be a minute's silence before the game begins, and it will be dedicated to him.

The MJHL has two other First Nations teams—the Southeast Blades, from Pine Falls, a couple of hours northeast of Winnipeg, and the Waywayseecappo Wolverines. The Wolverines, from a reserve northwest of Winnipeg, near Russell but still well south of The Pas, are the opposition tonight and tomorrow.

Their governor is a forty-one-year-old single mother and chicken farmer, Cindi Berg. The Wolverines play in a new arena on the reserve with a capacity of about 1,500; a hotel is attached to it. Berg says the regular-season crowds run between 400 and 500—lower than the OCN Blizzard's but much larger than the Winnipeg teams attract. Her team's budget is about $300,000. "We can't keep up with the Blizzard," she says. "They have more money than we have and they spend more."

Berg is white, but she has spent her life in the region, and all the employees at the chicken processing facility she runs are from the reserve. "So I kind of got involved in hockey that way," she says. She's also "a billet Mum," and seven of the Wayway players currently live in a house she owns. "It's really interesting," she says. "They're from all over, some even from the States. They'd never been up here before."

The franchise is into its fifth year. Two years ago the chief, Murray Clearsky, was replaced. "The franchise went into the gutter for a couple of years," Berg says. "But last February he was re-elected so we're redoing the team—new board of directors, new GM. I guess it's an image change. I think we really need this program in their area."

The crowd in The Pas is a bit smaller than last night's, maybe five hundred. "We're still the best draw in the league, though," the ticket taker says. "But it's so goddamn nice out tonight I guess people are outside doing other things."

Two of the players are doing other things, too. Paul Wallmann and Taylor Emmerson are among the spectators. They've been suspended for two games for their part in last night's brawl. Fighting isn't banned in the MJHL unless it extends to more than two fights at the same time, and last night it did.

Wallmann is the player to whom Coach Watson gave hell yesterday morning for not showing up for his job.

"It was cleaning car interiors and there wasn't enough work for me," Wallmann says. "That's why I quit." He smiles. "Glen's okay, but he's moody, grumpy sometimes." As for the fight, he holds out his right hand and says, "It's a bit sore, but it'll be okay." He also has an ugly bruise on his cheek. He is small for a defenseman, a slim 170 pounds. He grins and delivers the old line, "Its not the size of the dog in the fight, it's the size of the fight in the dog."

Emmerson, who is unmarked, is much bigger than Wallmann. He's from Abbotsford, near Vancouver, and has just been traded to the Blizzard from Williams Lake of the BCJHL. "I was disappointed, but after I got here I really liked it," he says. "The guys are great. Some people say it doesn't matter if the town is crappy because you're only here for the hockey, but the town is great." He doesn't have a job, either. He says when he's not at the rink, he's at the gym. "Hockey is a full-time job for me," he says.

Provincial Junior A players are eligible for scholarships to American universities because, unlike players in the Western, Ontario and Quebec major junior leagues, they aren't paid. That's why the bulletin board in the Blizzard's dressing room is peppered with cards from about a dozen of them, including Minnesota, Michigan State and the University of Alaska. Over the last two years, twenty-six players from the eleven-team MJHL have gone that route. If they're accepted they not only get an education, but they still have an outside chance at a hockey career.

Emmerson and Wallmann say they'll write the SAT, the American university aptitude test, in the spring. "They're more tricky than hard," Wallmann says. He says that Brown University (in Rhode Island), the University of Minnesota and Rensselaer Polytechnic, in upstate New York, have all shown interest in him and his brother, Mark, the center who has broken the hockey sticks.

Up in one corner, a middle-aged Native man is yelling down at three younger white men who are sitting at rinkside. The whites yell back. After one exchange, when all three turn and look up at him, the Native man yells, "You keep fucking eyeballing me like that and I'll come down and beat the hell out of you!"

In a second, he's out of his seat, down the steps, and has pushed himself in beside the three whites. All four sit and watch the game, chatting among themselves.

Back up in the corner another Native man is chuckling. "They're all friends," he says. "They were kidding." The second man's name is Abel Cook. He's a carpenter at the hospital and an ex–hockey player. "I played up until midget, and later I played for the Cumberland Cree. We won what they call the Indian Stanley Cup. It's a big tournament every year in North Battleford, Saskatchewan. Indian teams from all over. You gotta see it."

Cook says he goes to almost every Blizzard game. Between the first and second periods, two youngsters slide frozen turkeys along the ice at bowling pins. It was Wallmann and Emmerson's job to set up the pins. They do it good-naturedly. One youngster knocks them all down. The other misses them completely. However, the public address announcer says that he may keep his turkey, too, and the crowd cheers. The two suspended players then take the pins away, and a moment later the teams are back on.

Last year, Abel Cook says, he rolled a tire from center ice into the goal. "I won four brand new tires," he says, "worth $600." Just then he notices a pretty girl in a bright yellow-and-black windbreaker sit down with some friends a few rows over. "That's my stepdaughter, Alesia," Cook says. "She's only fourteen. She's a goalie in midget—boys' midget. You should see all her trophies. I'm gonna have to build a new rack for them."

Between periods, the three on-ice officials are in their dressing room. Unlike the players, they skate nonstop, apart from stoppages in play, for the whole sixty minutes, and it shows. Kelly Zarn is sweating hard. As he towels himself dry he says, "OCN is the best organization in the league. They treat us very well. The Pas is the best road trip we have." He says this even though he and David Marin face a seven-hour drive to Brandon after the game. They'll get home around midnight. The third official, Geoff Gregoire, lives in The Pas.

In the press box—a wooden balcony that can hold about a dozen people and tonight holds four—Burns Anderson is videotaping the game, as he does for all home games. Watson and the assistant coaches will go over them later. Anderson is a computer technician, forty-five years old, tall, easy-going, with a pinkish-white semi-punk haircut. His full-time job is at one of The Pas's two electronics stores.

He says he's been a hockey fan all his life and he works for the Blizzard for nothing. "I've always loved the game." His father was an auto mechanic who moved around. "So I've seen a lot of hockey, all over." He's lived in Toronto, Saskatoon, Nipawin—home of one of the Saskatchewan teams Ron Cox played against—Winnipeg and Comox, on Vancouver Island.

Another chore Anderson handles for the Blizzard is arranging billets for the team members who come from outside The Pas—which is to say, most of them. People billeting players get three hundred dollars a month for each.

"I never played hockey myself—I wasn't much on skates—but I have two sisters who played, played in boys' leagues, and one of them runs a hockey school in Comox. I came here twenty-seven years ago and I love it. My two kids were raised here."

Anderson's second wife, Sandy, whom he married up here after his first marriage ended, comes from Wisconsin. She's not quite so in love with The Pas. "I miss my family back home," she says. "I'd like to go back sometime."

Also looking down from the press box, taking notes and not missing a play, is Wayne Hawrysh, another of the assistant coaches. Hawrysh is from Dauphin, Manitoba. He came to The Pas to work in the Manitoba public auto insurance office and now has his own insurance-adjusting business. He was on those great Flin Flon Bombers teams in the sixties with Bobby Clarke and Reggie Leach. Gerry Hart, who played more than ten years in the NHL, mostly with the Islanders, was also on that team. So were Blaine Stoughton, who had two 50-goal seasons with the Hartford Whalers, and Gene Carr, who was with the New York Rangers and the St. Louis Blues.

Hawrysh is tall and gray-haired and wears glasses. He says his nose has been broken seven times. Unlike Jerry Mosiondz, he's never had it fixed, so it doesn't have much of a bridge left. Detroit drafted him in the third round in 1969. He spent most of his career in the Eastern Hockey League (which in 1973 split itself into the North American league and the Southern league) with the Jacksonville Rockets, the old Jersey Devils, the Cape Cod Cubs, the Long Island Cougars, and the Binghamton Dusters, before Binghamton joined the AHL. "Bobby Clarke's brother was the GM in Binghamton. You'd walk into the rink and think it was Bobby," he says.

"By that time I was twenty-five and my son was ready to go to school. It didn't look like I was going to make the NHL, so I decided to quit and come home and get a job. I could have gone back. Do you remember *Slap Shot*? I got traded from Binghamton to Johnstown [the team that, disguised as the fictional Charlestown Chiefs, was featured in the movie], but I wouldn't report. I didn't want to go there; nobody did. But I did know five or six guys who went there in trades, and they ended up in the movie."

One of Hawrysh's teammates in the Eastern league was John Brophy, later the Toronto Maple Leafs coach and since then a fixture of the East Coast Hockey League, the successor to the old EHL. "I sent a kid to Broph when he was coaching the Hampton Roads Admirals and he made the team. The next year I took two more players—our goalie, Lanny Pearson, and Cliff Duchesne—and we spent a week at the camp. I like being able to send kids on to something bigger than junior when their time comes, whether it's the East Coast league or Texas."

Duchesne is the young man who was killed in the snowmobile accident. He was billeted with Hawrysh when he played for the Blizzard. "He was like a son," Hawrysh says. Even now he has trouble talking about it. "We were in Winnipeg visiting our kids when we got the call about him, and the scariest thing was that when we got home there was Cliff's voice on the telephone answering machine wishing us a Merry Christmas. We were just devastated. You get so close to these kids. They're so far away from their homes and families."

Hawrysh looks back fondly on his own billets in junior. "I remember going to Flin Flon to play and going to live with strangers, and they treated me just like a son. That's one of the biggest things I remember about junior hockey."

As far as players go, Hawrysh says that Bobby Clarke is likely the best he ever played with or against. "And when you remember that Clarke is diabetic it makes it even more of an accomplishment. He was a leader right from the start. He'd get the guys going in the dressing room and he'd take it out to the ice. If he had an injury he'd suck it up and play—and the guys could see that kind of thing, eh? And they'd play hurt because they wanted to stay on the team."

Another player he feels strongly about is Guy Lafleur. "I grew up a Detroit fan—my Dad used to bird-dog [scout] for them," he says. "I didn't know or care about Montreal, but I got to know Lafleur through NHL old-timers' games, and he's one of the best guys I've ever met in hockey. Y'know, there wasn't a game we played, before or after, when he wouldn't sign autographs for any kid or anyone else who wanted one, no matter how long it took. He was fun, easy to talk to. You hear about players giving a hundred percent. Guy gave a hundred percent to the hockey public as much as he did on the ice. And with the team, he made everyone comfortable. I remember after our last game he threw me a pair of hockey gloves—good new Jofa gloves. 'Hey, Wayne, keep these if you want.' He was just a generous, nice guy."

Hawrysh feels strongly about his relationship with the Cree community. "It was very easy for me to settle up here," he says. "I grew up with a lot of people from the Cree side of the river. They'd been at residential school in Dauphin, so when I came up here I was running into old friends. I've always had a good rapport with the Aboriginal community and that was something that brought me to the hockey club."

He has no doubt that the team is helping to better relations between whites and the First Nations people. "Everyone picks up on it—writers, TV people, what have you. It sounds as if they're overdoing it, that it's a promotional thing they're trying to get the most mileage from. But there's no doubt that it has brought the communities closer together."

One of the things Hawrysh is most proud of is an eagle feather the Cree gave him for his work with the team. "It's the highest honor a non-Aboriginal can receive," he says.

The OCN Blizzard's season didn't have the splendid ending that seemed promised back in those glorious warm October days. The Portage Terriers knocked them out four straight in the first round of the playoffs and Glen Watson was fired with a year to go on his contract. "He was let go by fax," a man close to him said. "That was an unforgivable way to do it." But the trouble apparently began long before the playoffs loss. Around Christmas, two of the OCN players, with six or so other youngsters from the reserve, vandalized some ice fishing shacks. The hockey man said that when Watson wanted to trade the two, get them off the team, the band stepped in and the kids stayed. "That didn't sit well with the rest of the team," the man said. "I think that was part of the downfall of the club, that the players felt those two got special treatment."

Lou Personius, the OCN director, agreed that Watson had a good record but that he was fired because he did things without the band's okay. "He acted too much on his own," he said. As for firing him by fax, Personius said that was the only way they could reach him.

Watson said he's begun to hunt for another job—in hockey, of course—and didn't seem to be taking the firing badly. "We had our differences," he said. "Things just built up." But he was angry about the fax. He said he was away scouting. "They found out where I was and bang they sent a fax," he said. "You're gonna fire a guy, you don't do it that way. Getting fired is part of hockey. It's been done to me before, but not by fax."

CHAPTER 3

Hockeytown, U.S.A.

WARROAD, MINNESOTA • Warroad is on Muskeg Bay, at the southwest corner of Lake of the Woods, and it is much closer to Winnipeg than The Pas—only two hours and change. You go southeast on Highway 11, through orderly, well-tilled fields, past the tidy but busy Mennonite town of Steinbach, to the American border. Ten minutes more and suddenly, just off U.S. Highway 313, is the town's imposing water tower, with two crossed hockey sticks painted on it. In fact, Warroad is so close to Canada that its youngsters often drive to Steinbach for their hockey equipment.

This is hunting and fishing country. "Pan-fried walleye" is on just about every menu, and deer and moose hunting is a birthright. In the late fall and winter and early spring, hockey is as much a part of the soul and spirit of the cities, towns and villages of northern Minnesota as it is of Chicoutimi, Sault Ste. Marie, The Pas or Prince Albert.

And this long and storied love affair began years and years before the coming of the Minnesota North Stars and, later, the Wild. In the late thirties and forties, Johnny Mariucci, Mike Karakas and Cully Dahlstrom played for the Chicago

Blackhawks. About the same time, Frank Brimsek—the most exciting goalie of his time, who, like Mariucci, hailed from Eveleth in north central Minnesota—went to Boston. Since then, more than a hundred Minnesotans have played in the NHL, including the late Tommy Williams, who starred for Boston for years; Tom Kurvers, who played eleven NHL seasons; the New York Rangers' Mark Pavelich—not to be confused with Marty Pavelich from Sault Ste. Marie and Detroit; and Reed Larson, who had twelve NHL seasons, most of them with Detroit. More recent NHLers include Bret Hedican, Darby Hendrickson, Trent Klatt, Mark Parrish, Phil Housley, Matt Cullen and Jamie Langenbrunner.

Minnesota also produced two of hockey's most successful and innovative coaches, both of whom died too soon: Herb Brooks, of the 1980 "Miracle on Ice" team that won an Olympic gold medal for the United States, and Bob Johnson, late of the Pittsburgh Penguins.

Brooks also coached the New York Rangers, the New Jersey Devils, the Penguins and the North Stars. He died in a car accident in the summer of 2003. Johnson won Stanley Cups in Pittsburgh in 1991 and 1992; he died of cancer.

Brian Burke, the Vancouver Canucks general manager, who was born in New England but raised in Minnesota, says Canadians might sneer at the Johnny-come-latelies in Tampa, Atlanta or Anaheim, but they shouldn't when it comes to Minnesotans. "They know and love the game the way Canadians do," he says.

Although its population is around only 1,700, Warroad unabashedly calls itself "Hockeytown, U.S.A."

With its quiet, leafy streets, its neatly kept houses, lawns and gardens and its church spires, Warroad looks and feels like one of those American towns so loved by Norman Rockwell, the *Saturday Evening Post* portraitist—if you discount the sprawling casino on the waterfront.

At first glance, besides the water tower's hockey sticks, what distinguishes it from similar towns, whether in Connecticut or California, is the half-block-long building with its Olympic rings and "Christian Brothers Hockey Sticks" painted across it.

The Christian brothers are Roger and Bill, U.S. Olympic gold medalists in 1960 at Squaw Valley. Their company—whose motto was "Hockey Sticks Made by Hockey Players"—sold half a million sticks a year at its height. (The company closed in 2003, unable to meet stiff competition from bigger companies at home and abroad, as well as the new composite sticks.)

In all, Warroad has produced six Olympic hockey medalists, and there are likely more to come—which, for a town its size, is pretty good going. A generation after Roger and Bill's success, Bill's son, Dave Christian, was making headlines.

After playing on Herb Brooks's Olympic team, Dave spent nearly fifteen seasons in the NHL, largely with Winnipeg and Washington, scoring 372 goals in the regular season and playoffs.

The career of Henry Boucha, a 1972 Olympian and a first-round pick of the Detroit Red Wings, might have been as successful as Christian's, but it was cut tragically short. Boston's Dave Forbes butt-ended him in the face, blinding him in one eye. Boucha, a Native American, is back in Warroad, working in real estate and helping young Native Americans with hockey.

Besides its Olympic and NHL credentials, Warroad has a proud senior hockey legacy that includes three Allan Cups in a row. As well, four hundred boys and girls are in its minor hockey program—once again, remarkable for town its size. And its fierce high school hockey rivalry with neighboring Roseau (the hometown of the Broten brothers, Aaron, Neal and Paul, as well as Bryan Erickson and Earl Anderson, all of whom played in the NHL), goes back at least couple of generations.

Warroad's first indoor rink, which some called a barn, was built by Dave Christian's grandfather, a carpenter, and three or four others. They were paid for their efforts, and they worked during the day. At night, thirty or forty volunteers took over and worked for nothing. It was ready for the 1949–50 season. Dressing rooms weren't added until 1960; until then, players dressed in town and walked over. In the early seventies, artificial ice was installed.

The "new" Gardens, a gem of an arena that any Canadian town would be thrilled to have, was opened in 1993; it has an Olympic-size ice surface. "The NHL made a big mistake when it didn't go to the Olympic size," Bill Christian says. He's sixty-four, gray-haired, slim and soft-spoken. He's standing in the Gardens' spacious and spotless lobby, with its glass cases full of trophies and photographs and newspapers that celebrate Warroad's hockey past and present.

It's early morning and the arena is in semi-darkness. Christian waves his hand towards the ice. "The NHL owners are afraid of losing seats if they make the ice bigger, but it's going to come back to haunt them. People come out to see the skilled players, but there's not enough room, they're always being hooked and held. You hardly ever see an open-ice check;

just guys running each other into the boards. And they always have their fists up. They can't deliver a check without lifting their fists." He hold his hands up together in front of his face, almost like a boxer. Turning back to the rink, he says, "But if they're not going to make the ice bigger, they should at least take out the red line. For God's sake, open up the game."

Roger and Bill Christian live next door to each other, not far from the Gardens, where they often go to watch high school hockey. "There's not much else to do here in winter," Bill says.

Roger is sixty-eight and bigger than when he played hockey; like his younger brother, he speaks softly. He gestures towards the water at the bottom of their properties. "Sometimes when we were kids we'd have to lay planks across the open water so we could get to the ice to skate," he says.

Bill says, "The best place to skate was under the bridge over there, because you didn't have to clean off the snow. The only problem was that the sand they'd put on the highway in winter would spill over, so that made it hard sometimes."

The brothers say they still get a couple of letters a month, usually from Europe, asking for autographs. "They worship their Olympic athletes over there," Bill says.

The Christians are probably more familiar with Manitoba hockey than most Canadians are. Roger saw the Winnipeg Warriors play in the final for the old Western Hockey League championship. Winnipeg-born Billy Mosienko, who had just finished his Hall of Fame career in Chicago, was playing for them. "Some awfully good hockey players came out of Winnipeg," he says.

"Hockey used to be like one big family in the U.S. and Canada," Bill says. "Everybody seemed to know everybody else. That was good. It's not like that now—all the teams, all the players."

Roger agrees, but tells the story of going to a Chicago training camp. "They really gave me the cold shoulder because I was an American," he says. "The only guy they treated worse than me was a Frenchman from Montreal. But the trainer took me under his wing. I remember he said, 'Roger, you're not a drinker, are you?' I said no, and he said that when I went down to the tavern with the guys to switch to Coke or something after a couple of beers, but when my turn came, to remember to buy a round. He said that's all they care about—getting their round. After a couple of rounds, he said, they wouldn't notice if I were drinking water. The thing is, Bill and I played hockey all over Manitoba, and everybody got on fine. It was just with the pros. They were different."

Bill says, "We all had dreams of going to the NHL. I went to a St. Catharines Teepees junior camp one year. Rudy Pilous was the coach and manager there. I lasted one week and I was sent home. After we won in 1960 I went to Seattle in the Western Hockey League for a seven-game tryout, and then I was invited to their training camp in the fall. But I didn't make it. I wasn't in their plans. I didn't have enough talent."

The Christian brothers went to all the Jets games in Winnipeg when Bill's son Dave was playing for them. Roger says, "Something I'll never forget was the night a guy behind me kept yelling at one of the Winnipeg players, 'You're dumber than a Thanksgiving turkey!' I still laugh when I think of that line."

He ends with the observation that you don't want your coach to be your buddy. "It's better if you dislike him a bit," he says. "Then your attitude is 'The hell with you. We'll show you what we can do.' You end up playing your best just to spite him."

Hockey has been played in Warroad since the turn of the last century. Its godfather is Cal Marvin, for whom it is a passion. He's seventy-nine now, thin and in frail health. But when he talks about hockey, his voice becomes stronger and his eyes light up. "Warroad isn't going to send any boys to the NFL or the NBA," he says, "but a boy from here with a pair of skates and a good work ethic stands a chance of making the NHL."

Marvin was hardly back home from the Second World War—he went ashore with the U.S. Marines at Guam—when he began planning the team that would eventually become the Warroad Lakers. They lasted fifty years, until 1997, while senior teams in Canada died all around them.

"We couldn't always get the Canadians on side," Marvin says, referring to scheduling and travel costs. "But by the same token, without Canada we wouldn't have had any place to play."

The Allan Cup may have lost some of its luster since teams from Toronto and Ottawa or Montreal, Winnipeg, Edmonton and Calgary played for it. But it's been around since 1908 and still goes to the champion senior team. Senior hockey is on a par with the East Coast Hockey League or the Central Hockey League.

After years of success in various western leagues and tournaments where they won three straight Saskatchewan titles, six straight Manitoba titles and were Allan Cup runners-up, the Warroad Lakers won the Cup three years in a row—in 1994, '95 and '96. A run like that had never happened before. Not only that, but the Allan Cup had never been won by a team from such a small community.

The walls of Cal Marvin's sunny sitting room in his ranch-style house a block from the lake—as well as the house's hallways and kitchen walls—are papered with hockey memorabilia: photographs, programs, framed newspaper articles and plaques. Marvin is wearing a Warroad Lakers sweater. Through the window, his pickup truck can be seen; the dates of the Lakers' Allan Cup triumphs are painted on it. Behind him on the wall, one of the plaques, from the Pine Falls Paper Kings, recognizes Marvin's contribution to senior hockey in Manitoba. There are others from Canada, too.

But it's not only the Lakers that get Cal Marvin reminiscing. He and his pal, Dan McKinnon, an original Laker, were also behind the creation of the Fighting Sioux hockey team at the University of North Dakota in nearby Grand Forks. "We went to the athletic director and told him if he supplied a schedule, we'd supply the team. We went to the university, played for the Sioux and when we had a spare weekend we played for the Lakers," he says.

And he remembers well when UND first challenged the University of Michigan, a hockey powerhouse. "People were laughing at us, saying how badly Michigan was going to beat us," Marvin says, "but we upset them 6–5 in their own building." After the game, he says, a reporter wrote something like, "Until last night Michigan didn't know what side of the Mississippi the state of North Dakota is on . . . but they do now."

UND's hockey success continues. As the 2003–04 season gets under way, eleven former Fighting Sioux are on NHL rosters. They include Toronto's Ed Belfour and two veteran defensemen: James Patrick of Buffalo and St. Louis's Murray Baron.

Marvin says he wasn't a great hockey player himself. "My long suit turned out to be managing. I could go out and get the fellows." And over the years he did get them for his beloved Lakers—not only local players, but players from away, such as Bill Juzda, a defenseman who had played for the Toronto Maple Leafs and the New York Rangers and was one of the most feared bodycheckers of his time; Ed Kryzanowski, also a defenseman, who had played four full seasons with Boston; and "Sugar Jim" Henry, the Rangers and Bruins goalie. In all, over the years, ten Lakers had played in the NHL.

Chuck Lumsden is seventy-one and still lives in Winnipeg, where he was born. He never played in the NHL but he did make a Memorial Cup final with the Winnipeg Monarchs, losing to the Barrie Flyers in 1951. "I could have strangled Leo Labine," he says, looking back at one Barrie's best players and one of hockey's greatest pests.

Lumsden later captained the junior Toronto Marlboros and then played with the old Pittsburgh Hornets, the Maple Leafs farm team in the American Hockey League, for a couple of years. (A football career with the Winnipeg Blue Bombers—his brother Tommy was already playing for them—was cut short when his leg was broken in an exhibition game against Ottawa.)

"After a couple of years with the Hornets, [Leafs GM] Hap Day said I didn't figure in their plans, but he wouldn't release me, either," Lumsden says. "I wanted to come home and play for the Warriors. They offered me much more money than I ever got in Pittsburgh, but Toronto wouldn't let me. Day kept talking about the money they'd invested in me. I said, 'Money? You didn't give me any money. That's the problem.' I told him if anyone had invested anything, it was me—four years of my life." (Lumsden did manage to play in a handful of games with the Warriors before the Leafs forced him to quit. Among his Warrior teammates were some former and soon-to-be NHLers; besides Mosienko and Juzda, later a teammate in Warroad, they included Barry and Brian Cullen, both of whom played several years for Toronto; Eric Nesterenko, who played twenty years with Chicago and Toronto; and Fred Shero, the old New York Ranger defenseman and later a Stanley Cup–winning coach with the Philadelphia Flyers.)

The NHL had no jurisdiction over Warroad, so that's where Lumsden ended up. The Christian brothers were among his teammates. "They were really good," Lumsden says. "Warroad had a lot of good local guys."

He says that playing for Marvin was a privilege. "We just had a ball down there." He points out that Marvin did a lot to promote international hockey. "He was all over the map. When the Russians came, we played them; the Czechs, we played them."

"I just loved hockey," Lumsden says, and he can still laugh when he lists some of the things that happened to him. "I've had just about every bone in my body broken. I've had three concussions, two eye operations, broken nose, missing teeth, fractured cheekbone, broken ribs, broken hands, broken fibia, two knee operations, broken toes, broken ankles. You name it, I've had it."

Of Warroad, he says, "We played our hearts out. We hated losing a game. Cal was so good and got us into so many games. I hated to see it end, but it was about '68, I guess, and Cal kind of said, 'Well, Charlie, I think I'm gonna look for new blood.' I said 'Cal, go ahead. I've had a wonderful time. I wouldn't have traded it for anything.' I've a lot of good things to say about Cal."

Back in Warroad, Marvin pauses for a moment, thinking back to *his* love of hockey. He says, "Y'know, servicemen during the war could buy life insurance, and I had ten thousand dollars' worth. That was an awful lot of money back then. I told my mother and father that if I didn't make it back, the money was to go towards an indoor arena for Warroad."

Like his Canadian counterparts, Marvin has stories about the long bus trips—four or five hours to Dryden, Ontario, longer to Thunder Bay—the snowstorms, the scrambling for expenses, that sound like they're about hockey teams anywhere.

"We played all over," he says. "Anyone who wanted a game, we tried to play. I remember the Peguis team from a reserve north of Winnipeg asked us up for a game. A lot of people said, 'Don't go. They're a bunch a hackers; they'll chop you down. If you do go, make sure you get your money before the game or you'll probably never see it.' Well, we went, got our $500 for expenses, and Peguis even made the official we'd brought the referee. We had a great game and they treated us to a big feed afterwards—treated us like royalty."

Winning under Two Flags—the two flags being the Stars and Stripes and the Maple Leaf—is a history of the Lakers written by Warren Strandell, a longtime Minnesota journalist. "Cal's commitment and love for the game of hockey has been complete and without pay or financial reward," Strandell writes.

But Marvin could be strict. His love for hockey didn't blind him. Strandell quotes him as saying, "Hockey teams had a bad name out there in Saskatchewan, Alberta and B.C. It was hard to get rooms for the team. I was in the motel business, so I knew the problem. I always told our guys that if something was broken when we left the motel, the team wasn't going to stand behind it. Whoever was responsible would have to pay for it."

Marvin is opposed to sending professionals to the Olympics. "You've got to have heart," he tells Strandell, suggesting that the pros don't have it for the Olympics. He was particularly angry and disgusted when players on the U.S. team trashed their hotel rooms in Japan in 1998. "That really cast a bad shadow on hockey and the U.S. We didn't need that. The only thing that saved us in Japan was the women's hockey team."

Dan McKinnon, who is seventy-six, tall, bald and wearing glasses, can be found every morning having coffee at the American Legion. "Most of us had been in the service, so we went to the University of North Dakota on the GI Bill," he says. He, too, remembers well the game against Michigan. After graduation he played hockey in Sioux City, Iowa, and in California and Minneapolis. He won a silver medal with the U.S. Olympic team in Cortina, Italy, in 1956.

His hockey playing stopped in the fall of 1958, when he was thirty-one. "I was deer hunting and I was hanging a rifle from a tree and it went off and nearly blew my hand off," he says. "I was alone, so I walked a couple of hundred yards to the road and flagged down a car. I was sent to Winnipeg by ambulance. Five surgeons were there, and four of them wanted to amputate. The fifth wanted to try to keep it, and he did." He holds up his disfigured hand, wriggling the fingers. "And I can use it. The man who saved it was Dr. John Farr."

In *Winning under Two Flags*, Henry Boucha says: "We were rink rats. We'd be at the arena until ten-thirty or eleven at night and then we'd run home. For me, it was about a mile in the middle of the night. My pant legs would be frozen. We'd crawl into bed and then have to get up for school the next morning."

Boucha says he remembers going to the frozen river when Kenora would come to town to play the Lakers. "They'd fly in on ski planes—Sunday morning for a Sunday-afternoon game —and afterwards they'd fly back. That was quite a thrill, watching them."

Another old Laker quoted in the book is Gerry Wilson, a Winnipeg medical doctor. Wilson played junior in Manitoba and then moved east and played for the Montreal Junior Canadiens on a team that went to the Memorial Cup final in 1957, losing to Flin Flon. He even had three games with the NHL Canadiens on a line with Maurice Richard and Dickie Moore. He hurt his knee, however, and after he had recovered he was traded to Toronto. Wilson says Punch Imlach, the Leafs GM, wanted him to start with Hershey in the AHL. Winnipeg, at the time, had the Warriors in the old Western league, sprinkled with ex-NHLers like Billy Mosienko, Fred Shero and Al Rollins.

"I told him [Imlach] that if I was going to play in the minors it might as well be at home in Winnipeg," Wilson is quoted as saying. "He said that would be all right." But when he blew out his knee again, he turned to medicine. "I had a Grade 11 education and I didn't know if I could get into university, but I got in. I got my science degree and just kept going." He ended up as an orthopedic surgeon.

It was while he was at the University of Manitoba that he began to play in Warroad on weekends for twenty-five dollars a game plus expenses.

"When I got down there I was flabbergasted at how good the hockey was," Wilson says in the book. "I had thought I was going to waltz around in some recreational league."

However, the knee went again, and he finally packed it in. "I have kept a connection with Warroad through my practice. I saw a lot of Lakers. That includes Cal's sons, who either came up [to Winnipeg] as patients or brought somebody else up." All in all, Wilson says he's been involved in hockey in Warroad since the late 1950s—"Geez, that's forty years!"

But it hasn't always been a picnic on ice. "One day I'm in the emergency department at General Hospital and a call came through from Warroad saying that a young boy had been hit by a car," Wilson says. "And I find out that it was Cal's son. They were bringing him to Winnipeg. But fifteen minutes later, they called back and said . . . that the boy had passed away. It was just devastating."

Cary Eades is forty-three. He is the assistant activities (athletic) director at Warroad's high school and he coaches the hockey team. He comes from the Vancouver suburb of Burnaby. His father played for Seattle in the old Western Hockey League. Cary played Junior A in Penticton, British Columbia, and then for the University of North Dakota. One year, he says, his line, which included two other Vancouverites, was the highest-scoring line in the NCAA.

Eades is muscular and broad-shouldered, with short dark hair, a dark mustache and horn-rimmed glasses. An ugly, raised scar, like a piece of red rope, begins at his hairline and runs about ten inches down his back; that's where surgeons had to fuse shattered vertebrae. Eades had signed with the St. Louis Blues and was playing for their farm team in Salt Lake City when he suffered a broken neck. "It was December 26, 1983," he says. He was only twenty-two but his hockey career was over. Still, he feels lucky. He knows it could have been worse; he might be spending the rest of his life in a wheelchair.

"It was a pretty innocent play," he says. "I was coming in forechecking, and a defenseman ran a pick on me and gave me a little hook. I fell off balance into another player going the other way and my neck snapped. I was pretty bitter at first. I'd worked for it all my life and I thought I was knocking on the door of the NHL; then, in an instant, it's gone."

He says he wasn't paralyzed at first, but after his operation, while he was heavily medicated, he lost the use of his arms and hands. "I couldn't lift them for about three months. So, when you have to be fed, have your bedpan changed, your butt wiped, it's pretty dehumanizing. I learned to have a great deal of respect for people with a permanent disability. It was a good life lesson for me. Until then I'd taken a lot for granted. It made me appreciate a lot of things. Now I've closed that chapter of my life and opened a different one, coaching."

Eades won a national championship the second year he coached the Junior A team in Dubuque in 1992. That summer, he was at a celebrity golf tournament in Warroad, where he met the Christians and Herb Brooks and other hockey people. He and his wife liked the area, a job came up at the high school, and they decided to stay, at least for a year or so; that was ten years ago.

"Hockey is not only a tremendously exciting game because of the speed," he says, "it is unique, different from almost any other sport because of the skating. Skating is something else you have to master. Most sports are running or jumping. They're in one category. Hockey is in its own."

In the ten years Eades has coached, his high school team has won three state championships. He likens the caliber, at its best, to Canadian Junior B. Eades points out that in Minnesota there is mass participation in hockey until you are eighteen, and there are 155 high school teams, so the system gives a chance to late bloomers who elsewhere might have quit.

He says another plus is that players in Minnesota advance through all the levels—from peewee up to junior. He says that from what he knows about Canadian hockey now, the best kids skip levels, therefore missing important stages of development.

One of his favorite stories is about a visiting Ukrainian pee-wee team. "We beat them, but they didn't care about the score," he said. "They played fire-wagon hockey, I guess you'd call it. They didn't have positions: five people on the ice, go hard for thirty seconds and come off. They'd even change when the puck was in their end, and they didn't pass. They'd try to beat people. Afterwards I asked their coach, 'What the heck's with this?' He says"—and here Eades adopts a heavy eastern European accent—"'They skate first and get used to puck. Next year I teach pass. Tell me a good hockey player who skate and carry puck and can't pass, hey? Tell me. Next year I teach passing. Now, they skate.'

"I started thinking about it, so I told my coaches the next preseason that I didn't want them yelling 'Pass the puck' for the first week. I wanted the kids to carry the puck, go with it. Three days in, I couldn't stand it any longer. I stopped the practice and asked the team whether they'd heard a coach yell 'Pass the puck.' They said no, so I asked them, 'Okay, then why, when you get the puck, do you stop skating and start looking where to pass?' My theory is that the second they get the puck they hear those thousands of voices in their heads—the crowd yelling, 'Pass it! Pass it!'"

Youth hockey in Canada and the United States, he says, is overcoached and, by extension, that's why many of the European players seem so skilled by comparison. Something must be done, he says. "All the great goal scorers are a bit selfish," he says. "They know how to pass the puck, but they don't do it every time they touch it."

Eades says kids should have fewer games and more fun. "A lot of their hockey, from what I've seen, is for the parents' enjoyment, not for the kids," he says. "That's why there are so many games. Games are more interesting to watch than practices."

It's evening, and Dean McMillin is watching his thirteen-year-old son play "pond" hockey on the small rink adjacent to the Gardens. Ranging in age from about twelve to seventeen, a dozen or so youngsters, including girls, are chasing pucks around. They're all in helmets, but only three or four wear full equipment. Some leave, presumably to go home, and others arrive.

There's not an adult at rinkside telling them what to do, telling them to stop fooling around, yelling at them, "For God's sake, pass the puck!" They're just having fun.

McMillin points to a boy in jeans and a T-shirt he says is a high school senior. "He's unbelievable," he says. "His skating, his hand-eye coordination. I really hope he gets a chance to go on." Just then the boy spins, as if he'd been able to hear McMillin through the Plexiglas, and drives the puck into the upper right-hand corner of the net.

McMillin looks at his watch. It's a little after eight. "Some of these kids have been here since five o'clock and they'll stay till ten," he says. "They'll only come off every hour or so when they flood the ice. That's what makes good skaters and stick-handlers."

Cary Eades would approve.

CHAPTER 4

John Brophy

HARRISONBURG, VIRGINIA • John Brophy, with his thick white hair, broad shoulders and open, almost cherubic face—scars and all—looks about the same as he did when he was pacing behind the Toronto Maple Leafs bench fifteen years ago. But given his hockey career that stretched over more than fifty years and his reputation for being one of the game's most determined and pugnacious characters—as both a player and a coach—he's strikingly soft-spoken and easygoing. One reason for any change in him—and he's not sure there has been one—might be that, at seventy-one, he's grateful just to be alive. Heading for a golf game, in his beloved, native Nova Scotia, around five o'clock in the morning on a summer day in 2000, he was alone in his car when he fell asleep at the wheel and crashed; he was nearly killed. "Nova Scotia has a lot of rocks and trees," Brophy says. "I must have hit nearly every goddamn one of them."

That stretch of highway, near New Glasgow, a couple of hours northeast of Halifax, is usually deserted early in the day; but that morning, by chance, another car was behind him. "He called 911. He'd just arrived from Newfoundland and didn't know the area so he couldn't give directions to where I was, but they got to me," Brophy says. "I was lucky as hell. He said later that when he went down to the car to see how I was, I was moaning so loudly he thought it was the car's engine revving." Brophy's back was broken, he suffered severe head injuries and his face was banged up—including his left eye socket, so he's now blind in that eye.

In spite of the accident, once he's at a rink he's the old John Brophy. Home is Harrisonburg, in Virginia, but tonight he's two hours south of there, at the Roanoke Civic Center, home of the Roanoke Express of the East Coast Hockey League. He's sitting high up in a corner, the place where people who understand the game sit because from there they can see the whole ice surface. Below, the Express are playing the Florida Everblades. The ECHL, along with its forerunner the Eastern Hockey League, is where Brophy spent most of his career, playing and coaching.

The game has barely begun, but already the referee is upsetting him. He's called a slashing penalty that Brophy feels is questionable at best. A man passing by, carrying a tray of drinks in paper cups, says, "If you were still coaching, you'd be raising hell about that." Brophy nods, the man moves off, and Brophy says, referring to the referee, "Now look at him skating around, waving his arms, showing off. You'd think the fans paid to see him. Y'know, when I die and go to hell, the first person I'll meet is a prick ref like that."

The game's first ten minutes has three fights. Brophy has never said no to a good fight, so they don't bother him. What does are two offensive-zone penalties. "That's dumb hockey," he says. "I hate offensive-zone penalties. They'll kill you."

Harrisonburg, where Brophy and his wife, Nancy White, now live, is a quiet city of about 40,000 with a university and two colleges. It's in the Shenandoah Valley, southwest of Washington, D.C., in the heart of Civil War country—Confederate country. In 1862, in the Cross Keys battle in Harrisonburg, one of General Stonewall Jackson's senior officers was killed. It's a pleasant enough place to live, full of history and rolling fields, but it's horse farm country, not really hockey country, and Brophy misses his hockey.

Nancy, who comes from Prince Edward Island, is Brophy's third wife. They met in Toronto through Rick Fraser, the late golf and hockey writer, who was a friend of Nancy's and, like Brophy, a native Nova Scotian. Nancy is young, attractive, energetic and businesslike. She was one of Canada's best speed skaters but after missing out on a spot on the 1980 Olympic team by eleven one-hundredths of a second she took up golf in earnest. She says she was slugging balls into a net in Toronto when she caught the eye of George Clifton, one of Canada's best golf teachers. "My legs, from skating, were almost as big as my waist," she says. "I was so strong I could generate a lot of power in my swing."

Four years after she was taken under Clifton's wing, Nancy joined the LPGA tour. She stayed on it for eleven years. "I couldn't get over making a bad shot, though," she says. "We all do it, but you have to get over it. But I'd get down on myself and make things even worse." When Brophy was so badly hurt on his golfing holiday in Nova Scotia the couple were living in Lynchburg, just south of Harrisonburg; she'd been working there as a club pro, while he was coaching the Hampton Roads Admirals of the ECHL. (Hampton is on the coast, about three hours away, and the team would put Brophy up at a hotel there during the season.) Nancy had resigned her club job just before the accident because she planned to return to the LPGA tour. "But that didn't happen," she says. Instead, she ended up taking a year off from everything to help her husband recover.

When he was strong enough, after his surgery in Halifax, she had him flown for rehabilitation to the University of Virginia in Charlottesville. He was in a wheelchair for six weeks; Nancy was by his side through it all.

She says, "I'd go up every day from Lynchburg, about an hour-and-a-half drive, and stay until he'd had his dinner. It was particularly difficult at the beginning because of his head injury. I'd just get home and he'd call and beg me to come to get him. That was really hard. After he came home he'd go for therapy three to five days a week to the hospital in Lynchburg. He had to learn how to walk, and there was the mental therapy—speech therapy and occupational therapy and dealing with memory. It was really a very, very difficult year."

Early in 2003, with Brophy up and around again, they moved to Harrisonburg. There they own a Mulligan's Golf Center, where Nancy gives lessons and where there's a pro shop that likely rivals the best in the state. Brophy hits balls every morning around seven o'clock, before the place gets busy. "I used to be a seven or eight handicap, but now I can't hit my driver any farther than I can my seven iron—can't generate much power," he says. "I'm getting a bit stronger, though. My back will never be right, and walking up hills is tough, but I'm hitting them better."

Apart from a year out recovering from the accident, this is the first hockey season since the late forties that Brophy has been neither on the ice nor behind the bench. His rough-and-tumble career began as a teenage defenseman in the Maritimes and included nearly six years in the Maple Leafs organization— two and change as the Leafs head coach. That stretch of hockey ended last spring when he resigned as coach of the Wheeling (West Virginia) Nailers, also of the ECHL.

He misses hockey, particularly, he says, the challenge of getting his team ready for a game—"the competitive part—nothing is going to replace the excitement of that,"—but he seems content with his life. "I'm busy around here," he says of his work at the golf center with Nancy. A couple of times a month he goes to schools in Harrisonburg to work with youngsters playing roller hockey. "He likes doing that," Nancy says. Brophy adds, "And I can tell you one thing, when I get up in the morning nobody is going to fire me." He's laughing, but sounds as if he means it, too.

All in all, besides the Leafs, Brophy's coaching and playing career—he played until he was forty-one—took him to Halifax; Troy, New York; Moncton, New Brunswick; Baltimore; Charlotte, North Carolina; New Haven; Long Island; Philadelphia (in the EHL); southern New Jersey (the Jersey Devils); and Birmingham, Alabama. After that it was back to Halifax and the Nova Scotia Voyageurs. Next came St. Catharines, Ontario, when it hosted the Leafs' American Hockey League farm team, and then Toronto. His longest uninterrupted stretch was as coach of the Hampton Roads Admirals, in Virginia, from 1989 to 2000. (Among his players was Patrick Lalime, Ottawa's fine goalie.) He missed the next year in rehab after his accident, then came his two years with the Nailers. In all, from 1950 to

2003, it adds up to nine teams as a player, eight as a coach, seven leagues (three of which collapsed) and thousands and thousands of bus miles.

Brophy is proud of his coaching career. "I've probably coached or played in every rink in North America that has lights," he says. "I was in Long Island a long time and people began to notice me. I got better as a player and I trained like a maniac and I also hit hard—and you hit hard on Long Island and they love you. But, you know, although I wasn't that good a player, I must have been a good coach. I don't mean to boast, but I didn't start coaching until I was over forty and I got 1,027 victories—NHL, AHL, World Hockey Association and the Eastern league. Only Scotty Bowman's got more, and he started coaching when he was twenty-five."

Still, Brophy had a modest reaction when he won his thousandth game in the spring of 2002. "If you stick around long enough, they keep giving you jobs," he told a reporter, "so you got to win some."

Nowadays he doesn't get to as many hockey games as he'd like to. The Roanoke Express may be the team closest to Harrisonburg, but it's still two hours away, and because he can no longer see out of his left eye, he doesn't drive at night.

This night in Roanoke he's not dressed like a casual fan. He's in a dark blue suit, white shirt and a conservative tie. It's what he might be wearing if he were still coaching—coaches, as a rule, are pretty sharp dressers. And although Brophy never played for or coached the Express, fans, players and team officials in Roanoke greet him with affection, good humor and, most noticeably, respect. It's almost as if he'd brought Roanoke its first Stanley Cup rather than been a rival coach whose teams came in to try to beat the hell out of the home team. On this particular night, a cold and wet one, people press forward to shake his hand the moment he steps inside the arena. And it's not "Hi, John," or "How's it goin', Broph?" It's "Coach Brophy" or "Mr. Brophy" or, simply, "Coach."

In the hallway outside the Roanoke dressing room, a young man in his hockey underwear is getting the feel of a new stick. He looks up, sees Brophy, grins, and they embrace. "Jesus, it's good to see you," he says. He grins some more. "Yeah, I'm still banging them around." The player is Rick Kowalsky, from Simcoe in southwestern Ontario. He played his junior hockey in Sault Ste. Marie and is the Express's captain and one of its veterans. Then along comes the Express coach, Tony MacAulay, who also embraces Brophy.

MacAulay is only thirty-two and is in his first full season as head coach. He played for Brophy at Hampton Roads and, like Brophy, has a Nova Scotia background; he coached St. Mary's University in Halifax. They are old friends.

Soon, three or four other men are gathered around. The talk turns to a new ECHL rule that makes players wear half-visors. They don't like it because they say the players become careless with their sticks. "We have three or four guys missing teeth and a couple with serious mouth injuries, broken noses, because of high sticks," MacAulay says. Kowalsky adds, "Those visors have just made things worse."

Brophy nods. "Put a visor on a guy and suddenly he's a hero," he says.

Not one to play favorites, Brophy moves to Florida's side of the hallway, which is separated from Roanoke's by a heavy curtain. There he gets a warm welcome from the coach, Gerry

Fleming, who played briefly for the Canadiens and later coached in their organization in Fredericton and Quebec City. The Florida equipment manager, John Jennings, a Toronto native, is there, too. He and Brophy talk about the league's players and agree that most of them are just kids. "That's hard to remember sometimes when you get pissed off at them, because some of them are so big," Jennings says. "But that's what most of them are: kids."

They also agree that players from college are a gamble. "Sometimes their bodies shut down after forty games," Jennings says, referring to the shorter college schedule.

Says Brophy: "Another thing is, you never know how long a college kid will stay around. He may quit after a year and decide he wants to go into business."

After Brophy shakes hands again and goes up to find a seat, Jennings says, "Broph's a legend. It seems he's been around forever." Then he adds, "Broph's the only coach I know that used to get off the bus and help the guys unload, coming in at two or three o'clock in the morning. You gotta respect a guy like that."

Up in the arena, the Stars and Stripes hangs at one end and the crimson Maple Leaf at the other. An arrangement of the Stompin' Tom Connors classic, "The Hockey Song," whose chorus pays tribute to "the good old hockey game," is blasting out of the PA system. Brophy doesn't think it's actually a recording of Stompin' Tom. "It's someone trying to sound like him," he says.

A military honor guard leaves the ice after the national anthem. Brophy settles back in his seat and the line of well-wishers forms again. "You were a helluva coach," one man says. "That's what we need." Another says, "Coach Brophy, you gotta come back. The league needs you." Brophy accepts the compliments graciously. "Remember, I've been around this league for almost twenty years," he says, as the man moves off. "A lot of people know me."

A woman who looks to be in her mid-seventies, pushing an oxygen tank, its tubes fixed to her nose, says, "I just want to shake your hand, Mr. Brophy." A girl, perhaps twelve years old, and her father stand watching. As the woman moves off and the girl rocks shyly from one foot to the other, the father says, "Coach Brophy, would you sign my daughter's hockey card, please?" Brophy smiles and signs it. It's one from his days coaching the Leafs. "That's an old one," he says.

Brophy settles back again in his seat. He says it was a good feeling whenever one of his players in the minors made it to the NHL. "I mean, a guy is never going to make it unless his coach is pulling for him. Especially if he's on the bubble; he needs a coach talking about him, telling the NHL people how he can play." He adds, "You know some of the goalies who played for me in Hampton Roads?" And he names Ottawa's Lalime, Olie Kolzig of Washington, Atlanta's Byron Dafoe and Jan Lasak, who has played half a dozen games for Nashville.

The arena holds slightly under 9,000; it's about a third full. Brophy says that isn't bad, given the lousy weather, plus the fact that it's the Thanksgiving weekend—a time when many Americans stick close to hearth and home. "There seems to be a lot of young people here, which is good," he says, looking around. But generally, he's not optimistic about the future of hockey in a lot of places. The other night, he says, a sportscaster on ESPN reported on the firing of Bruce Cassidy as coach of the Washington Capitals. "Then the guy says that no one will care if there's an NHL strike or a lockout, that the Capitals could walk down Washington's main street in their sweaters and no one would know who the hell they were. That's what hockey's up against."

He goes on, "Most people don't give a damn about it. All most of the sportscasters do is make smart-ass cracks about the fighting—'Here comes the pro wrestling on skates.' Stuff like that."

But Brophy argues that fighting isn't the problem, it's that the game is losing its personality, at every level. "With the face masks, half the time you can't tell one from another. They're like a bunch of robots," he says. "They all play the same way, too. Shoot it off the glass to get it out—that's it. And when the defensemen get the puck at the point, they shoot it at the net and they [the forwards] crowd the net. That's about all they do."

He goes on: "It's a shame, because hockey players are the best athletes in the world. They have to skate—they have to use their hands, their feet, their heads. Hell, you might as well give your fridge a pair of skates as put them on a football player."

John Brophy was born near the Atlantic Ocean, in a farmhouse in Antigonish County, a couple of hundred kilometers northeast of Halifax. His mother died when he was an infant. His father went to British Columbia to work on the railway, so the children—four boys and four girls—were split up. Young John went to an uncle in Southside Antigonish Harbour, not far from Antigonish itself. "It was all fishing then," he says. "I remember being ten miles out in the Atlantic when I was nine years old—cold as hell. We were dirt poor, but at the same time I never lacked for anything, funny as that sounds."

And he loves stories from the forties and fifties about the old senior teams in the Maritimes. Sitting over lunch in a small restaurant in Harrisonburg, not far from the golf center, he says, "They didn't have much money, and whatever they had [after a game] they'd throw it on the bed and divide it up," he says. "It was all mines and steel, but the [Sydney] Millionaires, because of the steel, had more money than the others." And the legendary rivalry, bordering on hatred, between Sydney and the Glace Bay Miners on Cape Breton Island is as fresh to him now as it was then. He mentions a Sydney player, the goalie Nick Pidsodny. "In Glace Bay one night, they threw a bucket of piss on him," Brophy says. "A bucket of piss, for God's sake. That was what it was like when Sydney and Glace Bay played."

But his memories of Cape Breton aren't all about hockey. He loves to go to Baddeck. Not only does it have a fine golf course, but he likes to visit the Alexander Graham Bell Museum. "Bell did a lot more than invent the telephone," Brophy says, and mentions Bell's work for the deaf and his innovative projects, which included a hovercraft. Brophy misses Nova Scotia and says that if it weren't for the golf center he'd go back in an instant, back home to Antigonish. Then he pauses, frowning, and says, "Another thing, I don't like all the secrecy about the Iraq war. I don't think we're being told the truth down here, and that's not right." This is said with disappointment, but without a hint of sanctimoniousness; and it doesn't come as a surprise, because Brophy appears to be completely candid, a man without guile, someone who doesn't lie and doesn't like people who do.

Brophy is silent for a moment, then he returns to his Nova Scotia roots. He says he grew up idolizing an older brother, Tom, who went to St. Francis Xavier University in Antigonish. (Tom lives in Florida, and he and John are still close.) "Tom played football—it was rugby then—and was on a team that didn't lose a game in three years. That's where I got the bug for sports. It was hard, tough rugby, and I guess I wanted to be like him, so I guess I got my hitting from watching him play, only I did it in hockey. It was the only way I could play."

He chuckles and shakes his head, as if admonishing himself, and says, "I didn't go far in school. Maybe Grade 5. There was no one really to keep an eye on me. I know that one day we had a fire at the school—at least the alarm went—and we all went out and I got on my bike and rode down the road and never came back. Pretty stupid, I suppose, but that's the way it was."

All this comes without any bitterness or self-pity, either over growing up poor and without parents, or over the ups and downs of his hockey career, including being fired halfway through his third season with the Leafs. Looking back at it all, he can be serious, but also self-deprecating and funny.

Brophy doesn't order much to eat—just a small sandwich and a glass of iced tea. He speaks quickly but thoughtfully as memories flood back. "When I got older, I started hanging around the rink in Antigonish. St. FX used to have it all day— different teams, intramural, I guess, for an hour at a time. I got to know the guy who ran the rink, and I'd go over and sit, and they were always short players so I'd substitute and end up playing every game, maybe eight hours a day."

Finally, he says, he got to a hockey school in Halifax run by Ted "Teeder" Kennedy, the one-time Maple Leafs great. "I tried to get a pair of skates from the Antigonish Bulldogs, the senior team, but I ended up with a pair of different sizes. One skate was a size seven and the other a nine—something like that. But I loved to hit, even back then, and maybe I overdid it, because Kennedy said to me, 'Are you crazy or something?' Anyway, that's the way it started."

Later, Marty Barry, the old Detroit Red Wing, was his junior coach in Halifax. "I played three years for him," Brophy says. "One of the nicest guys you'd ever want to meet. He'd just look at me and shake his head."

Most of today's players stand over six feet and weigh more than 200 pounds, but even compared with the players thirty years ago, Brophy wasn't that big. When he played he stood five foot eleven and weighed around 175 pounds.

In the off-season he was an ironworker, which included stints on the DEW line—the Distant Early Warning radar line in the far north, which Canada and the United States built in the fifties, during the Cold War.

"And I worked all over New York, Long Island, and before that, when I was playing in Baltimore and Charlotte, I used to come home summers to Nova Scotia to work. I was a connector, a climber—when the steel came up I connected the beams. You start at three or four stories and work your way up. It never bothered me.

"But come the first of September I'd put away the lug wrench, shimmy down the column and leave. All that climbing and pulling made me strong."

He goes on, talking now about the punching bags that fighters train on. "And in the gym I was a heavy bag and speed bag guy. I could go thirty, thirty-five minutes nonstop on the speed bag. It was like nothing; and I could go nonstop for ten three-minute rounds on the heavy bag. You ask anybody: you gotta be in shape, you gotta be strong to do that. You see, when I played hockey I had the attitude that no matter who, or what team, we were playing, nobody, but nobody, could hurt me."

He says that of all the fights he had—and there were hundreds—two in particular stand out. "One was with Teddy Harris on his way up to the Canadiens. I was with Charlotte and he was with Philadelphia. He just stood there throwing. I was back against the boards. I thought I was up against Billy Conn." (Pittsburgh's Billy Conn came within a couple of rounds of beating Joe Louis for the world heavyweight boxing championship.)

"Then Bobby Taylor [who also played CFL football] and I had a stick fight. I was in a lot of stick fights, but this time I figured it was death, the way we were swinging. No helmets then. We were cut to pieces."

Brophy's survival-of-the-fittest hockey philosophy, which is likely outdated nowadays, may very well have helped him over his frightening car accident. It is simple and focused: you must be tough, mentally and physically, and you must never quit, on yourself or your team. An example of this, Brophy says, is Aaron Downey. Downey is with Dallas after parts of two seasons with Chicago. He played for Brophy at Hampton Roads before playing several years in the AHL. "This kid, when he comes to us, is playing Junior B somewhere [Cole Harbour, N.S.], and he can't even raise the puck," Brophy says. "But he tried harder than anyone else I know to make it. He went to the AHL and fought everybody, and then to the NHL and fought everybody. He made it strictly on desire.

"In hockey, if you don't have someone on your team to balance things out, they'll pick on your best players and run you right out of the rink. Your good teams are probably tough anyway, mentally and physically, and they're going to win. They're not going to worry about someone hitting them. But the other teams in the league may have only four or five good players. They got to have someone to protect them."

In spite of his reputation for embracing rough play, Brophy says he never ordered a player over the boards to fight. "One time, one of my players—I won't say who—got in a fight and tells the guy he's fighting that I sent him in to get him. So the guy skates right over and spears me in the groin. I was so goddamn mad. I told him it wasn't true, that I'd never do that. Why my guy said it, I don't know; maybe he needed an excuse or something. I never sent anyone to get anyone. You can see what's going on, and you might put players on you know can handle it, but it wouldn't be fair to a guy to ask him to do it. It's putting too much pressure on him. I know when I was playing no one had to send me out. I could see what was happening. I knew I had to straighten things out."

Next, Brophy tells a story about going to the United States for the first time. He was in Campbellton, New Brunswick, trying out for the old Atlantic senior league, when he got word that the Baltimore Clippers of the EHL were interested in him. "The people in Campbellton asked me where I was going with my skates, and I told them I was going home to dry them, but I jumped in my car and drove to Halifax."

He drinks his iced tea and laughs. "This is how things have changed," he says. "I got on the plane in Halifax on my way to Baltimore, and when I got to Boston I had no identification.

Not a scrap of paper saying who I am, not even a driver's license. I'm carrying my skates because I figured if I checked them I'd never see them again. This is the fifties, and the guy in Boston looks at me and says, 'You know you've gone from one country to another with no ID—like, zero?' I'm standing there with my skates, and then he says, 'Nobody, I mean nobody, can be that stupid, so this must be legitimate. Go ahead.' That's how I started in Baltimore."

Brophy says that among his teammates were John Muckler, who now is the Ottawa Senators GM, and Les Binkley, the goalie, who spent five years in Pittsburgh. They used to share a cab to the rink.

"One morning we're in the cab, heads down, probably having a nap, and the cab stops at the rink and we look up and there's nothing but foam—firemen's foam. The rink had burned down. Everything was gone—equipment, everything. I figured it was back to Nova Scotia for me, but no, they kept the team together and moved us to Charlotte, North Carolina. We played five games in a row there that counted as 'home' games, and the rest of the schedule, about forty games, we played on the road.

"In Charlotte they had a beautiful new arena. They didn't know anything about hockey that far south, but we sold out for all five games—packed the place, 10,000 a night. We didn't even have our own sweaters; we wore old Hershey Bears sweaters. Back then, even the best material wasn't anything like today. They were thick wool—they must have been the first sweaters Hershey ever had. We might as well have been wearing horse blankets, they were so heavy and hot."

Each story reminds Brophy of another one. He starts to

laugh. "There's the time I'm playing defense with Muckler, and Binkley's in goal," he says. "I guess Muckler and I weren't having a great night, because all of a sudden Binkley, in his high squeaky voice, calls out, 'Will you guys please, *please* get out of the way so at least I can see the puck?!'"

One of Brophy's early coaching jobs was with the Hampton (Virginia) Gulls of what was then the Southern Hockey League. The Gulls folded, but they'd had a working agreement with Birmingham of the WHA, so he went there as an assistant to Glen Sonmor.

The Bulls had Frank Mahovlich, who'd played on great Detroit teams with Gordie Howe and Alex Delvecchio; Rod Langway, who later starred with Montreal and Washington; Paul Henderson, Canada's hero in the 1972 series with the Soviet Union and the best skater Brophy has ever seen; and Mark Napier, who became a star with Montreal.

They also had what Brophy calls "most of the characters in hockey. And they were tough." Among them were the late Steve Durbano, who piled up more than a 1,000 minutes in penalties in 200 or so NHL games; Dave Hanson, of the movie *Slap Shot*; Frank Beaton, from Antigonish, who that year with the Bulls managed nearly 300 minutes in penalties in 56 games; and Phil Roberto, who went on to play for six NHL teams in fewer than eight seasons.

"I remember when Mahovlich joined us; Sonmor had him on the fourth line with Hanson and Beaton, who were hardly magicians with the puck," Brophy says. "Frank hadn't been doing much, and one day at practice a reporter asked what was wrong; and Frank thinks for a minute and says, 'I don't know, but I seem to play a lot better with Howe and Delvecchio.'"

Still talking about the WHA, Brophy says, "Foreign-born players should build a statue to honor Ulf Nilsson," the old Winnipeg Jet and New York Ranger. "Guys were always going on in the locker room about getting the goddamn Swedes, stuff like that. He just took it and kept on playing. Jesus, he was good. That Winnipeg power play with him and Anders Hedberg [later a Ranger, too], Bobby Hull and [the late Lars-Erik] Sjoberg on defense was probably the best in hockey."

The next year, Brophy succeeded Sonmor as head coach. The team was owned by the young John Bassett, whose father, also named John, used to be a part owner of the Maple Leafs. Brophy says that at the NHL meetings that spring, Bassett told him that he'd sold Langway to the Quebec Nordiques, Kenny Linesman to the Edmonton Oilers and Napier to the Canadiens.

"'Jesus,' I'm thinking, 'there goes the whole team.' But Bassett says don't worry. He tells me he's gonna sign all these underage juniors. Underage juniors to replace those guys?"

Those underage juniors, it turned out, included Rick Vaive, who later scored nearly 450 NHL goals—most of them for Toronto, where he was captain for five years; Craig Hartsburg and Rob Ramage, two of the best defensemen of their time; Gaston Gingras, also a defenseman, who became one of the NHL's best skaters and owned one of its hardest shots; and Michel Goulet.

"Goulet was only eighteen when he came, and he didn't speak a word of English," Brophy says. "He was a super player. He did everything he was asked to do. He became not only one of the best offensive players in the NHL, he became one of the best defensive left wingers as well. He scored more than 500 goals and he had to quit early because of concussions.

"With those guys, Birmingham changed from being one of the toughest teams in the history of hockey to a team that was all skill."

Earlier, Vaive had left Prince Edward Island to join Sherbrooke of the Quebec Major Junior league and scored 127 goals over two years playing what he calls hard, "in-your-face" hockey. "I must have been a pain in the ass to play against," he says. "I could have had two more years of junior, but what did I have to prove? So I went to Birmingham, and Broph reinforces my playing style, and I go, 'Hey, I'm right. I gotta keep playing that way.'" He goes on: "Obviously, talent comes into play, but talent alone is not going to get you to the top. You have to have a good work ethic, be ready to stick your nose in. I wasn't that big—six feet, six foot one, about 175 pounds—and I'm only nineteen and I'm playing against men. I'll always remember Broph saying that there'll be guys on the team to back you up, but sooner or later you'll have to stick up for yourself. I had 248 penalty minutes that year and had the snot kicked out of me a few times, but it helped me."

Vaive calls his season in Birmingham one of the best years of his life, and he tells the story of a particular player who drove Brophy to distraction. "He was pretty skilled and he was also one of those guys that just enjoyed life," Vaive says. "Nothing seemed to bother him. But what got to Broph was that he'd go down his wing, dipsy-doodle and then cut in to the middle. John told him one game, 'You cut in to the middle again and you won't play.' Well, he did, and John benched him for a couple of shifts. Then he gets back on and does it again, cuts in to the middle, and this time you can hear Broph all over the building yelling—at the other team's defense—'Somebody hit him, for Chrissakes, somebody hit him!' He wanted to teach him a lesson."

And there's the story of Wayne Dillon. He had played for Bassett when the team was still based in Toronto, then jumped to the New York Rangers after a couple of big years with the Toros. After the 1977–78 season, during which Dillon saw minor-league action in New Haven, he no longer seemed part of the Rangers' plans, and they allowed him to join the Bulls.

"I guess he was upset to be going to the minors," Brophy says. "Anyway, he didn't show up for a morning skate and I gave him hell. He told me that he hadn't come because he'd dreamt that the league had folded, so he didn't bother getting out of bed."

Dillon's dream wasn't too far off the mark; the next year, the WHA did fold. Birmingham moved to the Central Hockey League and Brophy coached there for two more years. Then the Canadiens came looking for him. "That was a big surprise, because Montreal never went outside their own organization for anyone," he says.

According to Brophy, Ron Caron, a veteran Montreal scout and later the St. Louis GM, was impressed by what he'd done with the Birmingham youngsters. "So I phoned the Canadiens and I finally got through—I guess it was like calling the Russian consulate—and the GM, Irving Grundman, told me to fly up. I met him in a room with a huge, long table—just the two of us, him at one end of the table and me at the other."

Grundman offered him the coaching job with Montreal's AHL farm team, the Nova Scotia Voyageurs, who played out of Halifax. Brophy says, "I asked him how much money, and the money wasn't bad, so I said, 'American or Canadian?' and he said Canadian. 'We're in Canada now. Go outside and think about it.'

"Well, I'd already thought about it, but I went outside. Did you ever see the movie *Major League*, where the guys are all dancing? That was me outside Grundman's office, dancing. Jesus, Nova Scotia was home. I thought I'd died and gone to heaven."

Here, Brophy laughs again and says, "Let me tell you something about being wanted by an NHL team. Once I was in Texas. I probably shouldn't have been there, but I was visiting someone, and her phone rang. It was for me. How the hell anyone knew where I was I don't know, but they found me. What I mean is, if they really want to find you, they'll find you, no matter where you are. If they don't, you can be sitting under their goddamn feet and they won't even look at you."

Brophy was in Halifax for three years and had a winning record, but when the Canadiens moved the team to Sherbrooke in 1984, he didn't go with them. "I wasn't French, and they needed French there," he says, again without a trace of bitterness.

Instead, that fall he joined the Leafs organization, which led to his becoming head coach. He began as an assistant coach under Dan Maloney and then went to the Leafs' AHL farm team, in St. Catharines in those days, as head coach.

"Then I got the job of all jobs," Brophy says. "Coach of the Toronto Maple Leafs."

Among Brophy's favorites, besides Vaive, were Wendel Clark and the Czech player, Peter Ihnacak. "He was strong and quiet and did the best he could every night." And there was Borje Salming, the great Swedish defenseman. "He was all heart," Brophy says. "If you asked him to play sixty minutes, he'd try to." He remembers clearly the cut Salming suffered that left his face so stitched up it looked like a ragged road map. "He was knocked down in front of the net, and a guy stepped back, right on his head. He was cut everywhere, all the way down one cheek, under his chin. He was lucky his throat wasn't cut or his nose chopped off, that some nerve wasn't cut. He got up off the ice, grabbed his face, put his head down and skated off the ice, skated off all by himself."

Vaive, who went to Chicago in the trade that brought Eddie Olczyk to Toronto, says many people have the wrong perception of Brophy. "They think that all he wants is tough hockey players, that he wants everybody to play a certain style. That's not true. I never heard him ask any of the highly skilled players to fight or bang and crash, that sort of thing. He just wanted them to play as hard as they could. John is an emotional coach. He's a Maritimer, and Maritimers are passionate about what they do. He played that way, still holds the record for the most penalty minutes in the Eastern league, and his attitude to playing carried over to his coaching. He was very fond of, very close to all the young guys he had in Birmingham. He helped us a lot, and I think the reason he liked us is because we all played hard. Because he wouldn't settle for less than a hundred percent, some people misunderstood him, and that's why he had some problems [with the Leafs], but it wasn't his fault. The problem was with some of the players. I love the guy. I loved him as a coach and off the ice. I still talk to him. He really cares about people. He's a good person."

In spite of being fired by the Leafs, Brophy can still laugh about certain things that happened during his time in Toronto.

He lived in an apartment building on King Street West, opposite the Wheat Sheaf tavern. The Wheat Sheaf, which boasts that it is one of Toronto's oldest watering holes—and looks it—is certainly its most venerable, and is popular mainly with sports fans.

"We were playing like horseshit then," Brophy says, "and I'd come out every day and the Wheat Sheaf would be flying this huge banner. It said, 'New Diet—Eat Only When Leafs Win!' The way we were playing, you'd be skinny in a hurry. I finally went in and said, 'Will you please take that goddamn thing down?' and they were laughing. I can't remember whether they took it down or not, but it was getting pretty ragged by then anyway."

He goes on. "Then there was the Bobby Orr Skate-a-thon at Maple Leaf Gardens around Christmas, and the place was full of kids. I'm skating around, and one little kid calls out, 'Y'know you're fired?' He was right, even if he was a bit early. Anyway, before I know it there are headlines in all the papers saying the Leafs better win or I was gone. The next game is against Pittsburgh, and they were loaded then. Well, before you know it [Tom] Barrasso lets in a couple of soft goals, then another. When the period ends, [Paul] Coffey is so mad he jams his stick into the radiator of the Zamboni so they can't flood the ice, and he's kicked out for the rest of the game. Then [Mario] Lemieux gets hurt. In the third period Barrasso lets in five more goals and we win 8–5 or something. The papers are full of stuff about the team winning for me. I don't think so. I wasn't that friendly with any of them that they'd do something extra for me. They were playing for themselves, which is the way it should be. Three days later, Christmas Eve, I got fired."

Brophy's record that season was 11–20–2. His overall Leafs coaching record was 64–111–18.

Gord Stellick, now a sports broadcaster in Toronto, wasn't the Leafs GM when Brophy was hired, but he was when the coach was fired. "When I became GM in April '88, I accepted that Brophy was the coach," Stellick says. "I certainly liked him and I hoped it would work out. It was really tough letting him go." Stellick says it didn't help that he made what turned out to be a unpopular trade for Brophy. Russ Courtnall was one of the NHL's best skaters but, after three successive 20-plus goal seasons, he had only 2 points in 9 games. He was sent to the Canadiens in exchange for the thuggish, and later severely troubled, John Kordic, whom Brophy had got to know when they were both with Montreal. Six weeks later, Brophy was gone. Kordic ended up playing 104 games for the Leafs over parts of three seasons, scoring 10 goals and being penalized nearly 450 minutes.

Stellick goes on to say that the very qualities that made Brophy a success with the young Birmingham Bulls and other minor-league teams are what may have hurt him in the NHL. For one thing, he says, "Brophy wasn't necessarily God to the NHLers. Some of these guys had multi-year contracts for much more money than their coach was making. He had a hard time with guys to whom hockey came more easily than it had to him but at the same time didn't like to get their noses dirty. He even said, years later, that he couldn't understand why people wouldn't do what he would to be in the NHL. I mean, he would have killed to be there."

Brophy says that Courtnall "had all the potential to be the great player he became, but he wasn't playing that well at the time for us. Kordic was booed, but then it turned out he had some other issues. It was too bad, because he was a nice kid."

And if Stellick is right that some players thought they were too good for Brophy's gung-ho attitude, others say the opposite. Olczyk, later a Penguins coach, says it was when he was traded from his native Chicago to Toronto that his career really took off. And he says Brophy's passion and intensity had its memorable side. "Once, in Minnesota, we were losing 4–1 after the first period," Olczyk told a Pittsburgh reporter. "After we'd got to the dressing room and he'd finished yelling at us, he started to walk out. He stopped at the door. 'You guys looked like you were asleep out there,' he said. 'So when you sleep . . . the lights are out.' He switched off the lights so we're all sitting there in the dark. After a while Salming switches the lights back on and in a second Broph's back, and he knew who'd done it—'It was you, you goddamn Swede, wasn't it?'— and off went the lights again."

Olczyk said Brophy would get so worked up he probably broke more sticks in practice than some players did all season.

Looking back, Brophy says he has no complaints about the way the Leafs treated him, that they are still his team and he's always checking on them, worrying about whether they have the necessary stuff to win the Stanley Cup. "I wasn't surprised when I was fired," he says. "You don't win games, you're gonna get fired. That's the way it worked. But I was disappointed I didn't do better as a coach for the team. That was what hurt."

He goes on, "I can always look back and say I'd do things differently. Anyone who has ever coached for a while has got to have stuff he'd like to take back. With me, it would have been better if I hadn't said certain things. I probably should have had a little more patience with the players. I mean, you're not a hundred percent right all the time, that's for sure. One thing I'd recognize is that players have feelings, too . . . I wish I'd spent a little more time getting to know all those kids better. The deal with me was that we had to win, had to win, had to win. Who'd you run over didn't matter.

"But any coaching job I ever had I figured I wasn't going to be there forever, so I did what I thought I had to do. Then, when you're gone, you can't blame anyone else."

Asked about his strengths as a coach, Brophy says he doesn't like talking about things like that. "I don't know," he says. "I guess I was a hard worker. I certainly tried to win every game. That's all I can say."

He also has no complaints about the Toronto media. "Coming through the minors, if you didn't have the media on your side you didn't have anyone in the rink, so when I was asked a question I always tried to answer it, to talk about the game as long as they wanted to—any publicity you got was good for the team. When I got to the Leafs I didn't do anything special. I was just feeling myself along, and I treated the media the way I always had. I just told the truth—I still didn't like picking up the paper, though, reading about myself, because I was always scared they might be ripping me. But you know what? I can't say one bad thing about anything that was written about me."

He took his last job, with the Wheeling Nailers, a year and a couple of months after his accident. "Pittsburgh was running Wheeling, and they sent me there to change things around," he says. "But if for two years you don't make the playoffs, I guess I wasn't changing too much. Pittsburgh treated me like gold, but I just figured it was my time to go."

He's quiet for a moment, but there's a sense he's not finished, and he isn't. His old passion for the game is bubbling again. "Wheeling should have made the playoffs the first year," he says, his voice rising slightly. "We were playing Cincinnati and we needed a win. We're leading 4–3 with two minutes to go and the referee calls one of our guys for playing with a broken stick. A broken stick is a stick in at least two pieces, shaft broken, blade off . . . Our guy's working the puck out along the wall. His stick never came apart. It was cracked, not broken, not a danger to anyone, but the ref calls him. I yelled at the ref, 'You think he's goddamn superman he can hold a broken stick together and still get the puck out?' Anyway, Cincinnati ties it with thirty seconds to go and they beat us in a shoot-out. That was the toughest loss of a point I ever had. It was so bad that if I'd started after the ref I would have had a heart attack. The next year I recruited well, but I just couldn't get them together. I got tired of pushing people up the hill when they didn't want to go . . . And that was two years I missed the playoffs and I'd never missed two in a row before . . ."

He goes on. "As a player, I guess I'd say I tried to hurt everybody out there. It wasn't very nice. But I paid a price, too—my nose getting broken, cauliflower ears, busted hands. But you see, when I was playing, you'd run into the dressing room before every game to see if your sweater was hanging up, because if it was, that meant you were playing that night, that you'd lived to fight another day."

As for suggested rule changes, such as banning fighting, Brophy says hockey should be left alone. "Let them police themselves out there," he says. "Let them play the game and get some of the old rivalries going—Toronto–Montreal, Boston–Detroit, the Rangers and Islanders. Now they're just a bunch of sweaters running around."

He doesn't want the red line eliminated, either. "Like basketball—you can go down and nobody's near you," he says. "You can go down and score and swing off the basket. Maybe they can take the red line out and the blue line out and you can stand in front of the net and score and swing on the crossbar. That what they want? Jesus, let 'em play the game the way it is."

Back in Roanoke, as the third period winds down, a young police officer walks over and says to Brophy, "I've seen a video of you down there on the ice having a disagreement with another officer." He's talking about a night in January 1999 when Brophy was coaching Hampton Roads. After the game, a fight broke out on the ice and Brophy was charged with assaulting two security guards. The guards said they were trying to keep him away from the Roanoke fans. Brophy pleaded guilty and was fined $1,000 and suspended for six games.

Without taking his eyes off the play, Brophy tells the police officer, "I wasn't very smart that night. I'm not proud of what I did, but they were throwing batteries at us when we were leaving the ice. There could have been a riot."

The young policeman is smiling. He says, "I know, I know, sir. I just came over to say how much I respect you—how much I've always respected you." He reaches for Brophy's hand.

Roanoke prevails over Florida, 7–5. Brophy returns to the hallway where the dressing rooms are and says his goodbyes, shaking more than half a dozen hands.

Outside, in November's cold and wet, it's more like Nova Scotia than Virginia. But Brophy, without even a light topcoat, doesn't seem to notice. For someone who fished in the North Atlantic before he was ten years old, whose toughness was later honed high up on steel girders and in construction camps, and who played and coached hockey up and down the east coast for nearly fifty years, a bit of bad weather isn't going to bother him. As he crosses the parking lot to the car for the two-hour drive home to Harrisonburg, he looks back through the rain at the arena. "That was fun," he says. "I enjoyed that."

Four months later, John Brophy says he was dumbfounded by Todd Bertuzzi's attack on Steve Moore. "You know, I've never seen anything like that—coming up from behind, grabbing the sweater, pulling him back. That was just awful, terrible. Mooresy's brother, Mark, played for me . . . They're not going out on the ice trying to hurt somebody. They play the game. I don't know . . . Bertuzzi must have lost his goddamn mind, that's for sure.

"You know the biggest thing for me? It was at the end, that Bertuzzi ever got out of the rink alive. I don't mean it like that, but I don't know what Colorado was looking at after that. He was skating around with his helmet off like nothing had happened. Why they didn't go after him, I don't know. I do know that [on ESPN's] SportsCenter, they don't say anything about hockey, but they played [the Bertuzzi attack] to death. CNN, all the major networks . . . you know, they don't like hockey anyway, and here's another black eye for the game."

Then Brophy wants the latest news on the Leafs, whether they are ready for the playoffs. He thought it was great that they'd picked up Brian Leetch. And he also wants to hear about Sidney Crosby, the country's most celebrated junior, who plays for Rimouski. "You know, he comes from Nova Scotia," Brophy says. "From Cole Harbour. That's good, eh?"

CHAPTER 5

Down Mexico Way

LAREDO, TEXAS • Jaime Fuentes is a Laredo business-man, but this evening he's out in a T-shirt, worn baggy trousers and a gray baseball cap. The cap's logo is the head of a deer, with full antlers. In other words, a buck. Underneath the buck's head are the words "Laredo Bucks." Jaime, in his mid-thirties, is standing with some pals in the huge outdoor parking lot of the Laredo Entertainment Center, under a black, starry sky, smiling at the world. The Entertainment Center is a two-year-old arena and home to the Laredo Bucks of the Central Hockey League.

A crudely painted sign beside Jaime says, "Bucks Booster Club." It's 6:45. The Bucks game against the Rio Grande Valley Killer Bees starts at 7:30, and Jaime is with some pals. They're standing around a barbecue by their car, cooking faji-tas and Mexican burgers and chicken legs and offering them to any of the fans who are streaming towards the arena. These fans are in a pretty good mood; not only are they going to a game that they're catching on to, but their team generally wins. And as well, they're dressed in light sweaters and short-sleeved shirts for the first time in about a week. Laredo's weather, which has been like Rouyn's or Red Deer's in November, is now back to where it should be for mid-February on the Mexican border in south Texas.

Along with the cooked stuff, Jaime is passing out beer in frosted brown bottles. "It's our tailgate party," he says. "No charge. We do it before every game." Unfortunately, Jaime won't see tonight's game. He has to leave before it starts to go home to change. It's Valentine's Day, and he's promised to take his girlfriend out, and a hockey game isn't her first choice. "This will be the first one I've missed, the first home game, ever since they started," he says. "That's a year and a half." Sounding proud of himself, he says again, "That's a year and a half, every home game, since they started."

Seventeen teams—some of which used to be in the Western Professional Hockey League, which is no more—are in the CHL. They stretch from Hidalgo, in the Rio Grande Valley—which, like Laredo, is on the Mexican border—all the way to Indianapolis in the north. Nine of the teams are from Texas. Among them are the Amarillo Gorillas. Amarillo is the old cowboy and cattle town that turned to munitions and assembled the atomic bombs that were dropped on Japan in 1945; Corpus Christi, whose closest connection to hockey until now is likely that it's the birthplace of the longtime New York Ranger (and now Maple Leaf) Brian Leetch, although he didn't stay around long—has the Rayz; and the Cotton Kings from Lubbock, the hometown of rock legend Buddy Holly.

So when the NHL's Dallas Stars, the Houston Aeros and the San Antonio Rampage of the AHL, and the (Beaumont) Texas Wildcatters of the ECHL are counted, Texas has twelve professional hockey teams. That's more than in any other state, or any province. Then there's the twenty-one-team North American Hockey League, a Tier II Junior A league in which most of the players are shooting for college scholarships. It has four Texas teams.

Like the Ottawa Senators' Corel Centre, the Laredo Center seems to shoot up out of a field in the middle of nowhere—although in Laredo there's some cactus among that nowhere—surrounded by acres of parking and not much else. But downtown Laredo is only minutes away—unlike in Ottawa, where a trip to the Corel seems like a drive halfway to Kingston. And they're getting on with development around the Laredo Center—houses and shops and schools—again unlike in Ottawa's suburban wasteland.

The arena's capacity is 8,000. The Bucks average around 6,000, which is more than okay, particularly when, as coach Terry Ruskowski points out, the Bucks have the fewest weekend home dates in the league. For a city like Toronto, this size of arena would be ideal for its second team, the AHL Roadrunners, except that its comfort and roominess might spoil the fans.

At his tailgate party, with its beer and chicken legs, Jaime Fuentes says he didn't know anything about hockey until a friend in Los Angeles took him to a Kings game. "I fell in love with it whenever I got the rules straight," he says. A second young man standing by, Martin Infante, says, "This is soccer country. And hockey's like soccer, only on skates and with sticks and fighting. It's great."

A third man, Garry Cervantes, had reservations at the beginning. He says he was against the proposal to build the arena when it was put to a city vote. He and many others wanted a baseball or soccer stadium instead, and he says their side almost won. "They tried to force-feed us hockey early on, but now that it's up and going I'm really pleased. It took off like wildfire," he says.

And why not? The Bucks made the CHL's semifinals in their first season and in this, their second, they are way ahead in the league standings. But Garry makes a cautionary observation. "Yeah, right now we're winning all the time, so it'll be interesting to see what'll happen if we have a losing season. I'd like to see that. That's the test, when the novelty and winning wears off."

Upstairs in the press box, Joe Dominey, who handles the Bucks' play-by-play on "Classic Hits 94.9: The New QURE-FM," is setting up for his broadcast. He's a hefty thirty-one-year-old with a goatee and a shaved head who got into the hockey business in Seattle. Along from him is Luis Villarreal, a slim, dapper man who does play-by-play in Spanish for Amigo Broadcasting. Hockey isn't totally new to him: his wife's family came from Canada and his brother-in-law played hockey at Fargo State University in North Dakota.

Amigo carries seven games a year. "All we're getting so far is street comment, no hard figures on listeners," Luis says, "but so far it's been pretty good." He says that in his broadcasts he tries to liken hockey to soccer. "You know, where hockey has a fixed offside, in soccer the offside moves, but they understand what it means. When it comes to 'icing,' I call it 'icing.' There's no Spanish word for it."

Luis says he doesn't try to use colorful hockey words or phrases because, translated or not, they wouldn't make sense.

"You know, like 'top shelf,' 'slapshot,' 'stickside,' but 'passing' and 'checking' are fine because they're in soccer. But I try to keep it simple. I don't guess at something I don't know."

He estimates that at least 20 percent of the hockey crowds, including 600 season-ticket holders, are Mexican, crossing from Nuevo Laredo for the games. "And that doesn't count Hispanics on this side," he says. "Remember, you stand a better chance in Laredo of meeting someone who speaks Spanish than speaks English."

This season the Bucks lineup has been a challenge for Ruskowski, a forty-nine-year-old native of Prince Albert, Saskatchewan, who has been around hockey—NHL and otherwise—since he was a youngster, and knows what he wants. The Bucks are leading their division easily, but in all professional team sports players must come and go, answering to injuries, and, in the minors, to call-ups—in Laredo's case, to its AHL affiliate, the San Antonio Rampage. On this winter weekend Ruskowski has to go with only fourteen skaters. (He has been down as low as ten.) His players are all Canadians—graduates of junior hockey, major and otherwise, or university hockey— except for a Swede and an Israeli. (The Israeli, Max Birbraer, comes from Kazakhstan and played there with Nik Antropov, the Toronto Maple Leafs forward; Birbraer also played Tier II junior in Ontario.)

Depending on their status and any agreement they might have with an NHL or AHL team, the players make between $300 and $1,000 a week. Their apartments and utilities—hydro, cable and the rest—are paid for.

But whether they're staying put in Laredo or moving up, injured or playing, they know at least that the winter climate, even when it's bad, has got to be better than it is back home. As well, the people are friendly, there's lots of golf and, except for when there's an evening game, their day is usually over by about 1 p.m., when they've showered and dressed after the morning practice.

"It's hard to beat the hours," says Bobby Chad Mitchell. Mitchell is from Nipawin, about an hour east of Prince Albert, and he plays left wing. He's a twenty-one-year-old with red hair and that ubiquitous wispy goatee that seems as much a part of the young hockey player these days as his skates. At six-two and 245 pounds, he's the Bucks' biggest player. Although he doesn't score much, coaches love him because he never quits. He also takes a lot of penalties. And, as the sketch of him in the program points out, in December, playing against Lubbock, he got the Gordie Howe hat trick—a goal, an assist and a fight.

Mitchell played four seasons for the Moose Jaw Warriors in the Western Hockey League and one more in the Saskatchewan junior league. Right now he doesn't know what lies ahead for him beyond Laredo, but in an age often characterized by selfishness, cynicism, greed and discontent, he's having fun. Asked whether he likes playing in Laredo—this is his first year—he seems astonished by the question. "What do you mean, like? I love it." He's grinning broadly. "Hey, look, it's gotta be better than fifty below and having to work for a living, eh?"

Nearly 200,000 people live in Laredo, smack on the Mexican border, about three hours due south of San Antonio on Highway 35, and six hours southwest of Houston. If you fly in, from Dallas or Houston or anywhere else, you land at Laredo International Airport, which is new and spacious and has free parking.

Out in front is a big statue in bronze of a cowboy and his pony.

Laredo's Spanish heritage is evident in its churches, its squares, its walkways, in the wrought-iron grillwork that seems everywhere, and in the cattle ranches, some of which have been around since Spanish rule. And, as Luis Villarreal says, there's more Spanish spoken in the streets than English. But Laredo is not rooted in its past. The Chamber of Commerce says Laredo is the fastest-growing city in Texas, and the second-fastest-growing in the country. Across the Rio Grande in Mexico, Nuevo Laredo, which amounts to a twin city, has another half a million. It's a busy few square miles. The two cities' broad, straight streets and *avenidas* and expressways are jammed with transport trucks, many of them from Canada; thanks to the North American Free Trade Agreement, they're packed with thousands and thousands of tons of goods. An estimated 40 percent of all U.S.–Canada–Mexico truck trade goods are moved to and from Mexico, all day and all night. Huge warehouses full of more freight awaiting transshipment line the highways around Laredo.

Julian "Kiki" DeAyala, who owns the Bucks with Glenn Hart, a Houston oil-and-gas man, is confident that hockey won't go the way of baseball—the AA Laredo Apaches didn't make it out of the nineties, and Nuevo Laredo's Mexican League baseball team had to move to Tijuana. "We're doing well down here," he says. That's why he's gambling on an arena football team, the Laredo Law, that begins play this spring. (The Law's head coach, Scot Maynard, was wide receivers and special teams coach with Winnipeg when the Blue Bombers won the 1990 Grey Cup, and later did the same job with the Toronto Argonauts.) DeAyala calls Laredo the "biggest inland port in the country. And we have banking, real estate, natural gas and some cattle ranching."

DeAyala is forty-two, broad-shouldered, probably goes about 230 pounds of muscle. Sitting in his office at the Laredo Center he looks too big for his chair, looks as if he could still be the pro football linebacker that he was. After being chosen as an All-America at the University of Texas, he played for Houston in the now-defunct United States Football League and then with the NFL's Cincinnati Bengals. But at only twenty-seven he had to limp away from the game because, he says, his body was getting too broken up. That's when he went back to Houston, made a packet of money in real estate, and began investing in professional sports.

He's also a hunter and fisherman. On his office walls are the mounted heads of two deer, the skin of a six-foot rattlesnake and something he says is a "Rooster Fish," whose long, high dorsal fin looks like a rooster's comb. The fish is about four feet long. "I caught it in Mexico," he says.

He and his partner were happy enough with their hockey investment in Houston, with the Aeros of the International Hockey League (the IHL was absorbed by the American Hockey League in 2001), that they invested $15 million to build three state-of-the-art rinks so that Houston youngsters could get into hockey. All this made them confident that hockey would work in south Texas. But Laredo was another matter. "We weren't sure what would happen here, but we did know that the only sport out there that had been successful in a market this size was minor-league hockey," he says. "And we also knew that if an arena were built it would need an anchor tenant. We've brought in kids with good character to play for us, and Coach Ruskowski does a great job, on the ice and visiting hospitals and churches and talking to schoolchildren. The people in the community love him."

"I've been better treated here than anywhere," Ruskowski says. "You go into a grocery store and, it's 'Congratulations, coach, you're doing well, coach.' It's a great feeling. I don't want to let the fans down. I want them to be proud of us, on and off the ice."

At practice this morning, Ruskowski had the team working on the neutral-zone trap. Twice he called the players over to the play board, where he marked out what he wanted done.

Afterwards, in his small office, which is just off the team dressing room, he says, "We try to nullify their power when they're bringing the puck out, prevent the pass from D-to-D [defenseman-to-defenseman]. And we try to take the boards away, and our winger comes to center to take away the cross-ice pass, so they've got nowhere to go. My philosophy is that if they have no chance to make a play, they won't make a play. I like to get on them quick. There are two ways of doing it, but we weren't doing it right; so instead of yelling and screaming, I go back to the board and I say, 'This is what we do.' And then if they don't do it right I bring them back to the board again. If they still don't do it right, *then* I start yelling." But he doesn't swear.

Counting the time when he played junior, Terry Ruskowski has been in hockey, as a player and coach, for more than thirty years. He occasionally refers to God and prayer, but it would be a mistake to think of him as some kind of pious softie. He expects a lot from his players and can be as hard on them as any coach. And although he played at five-foot-nine and under 170 pounds, he collected nearly 800 regular-season points over fourteen seasons in the NHL and the World Hockey Association—and more than 2,000 minutes in penalties.

"He was a tough little monkey," says John Brophy, the former Toronto coach, who remembers Ruskowski from the WHA. "He'd stand in there with the best of them. When he was playing for Winnipeg, he was major."

"I was on some teams that weren't so brave, so often it was up to me," Ruskowski says. "My last year in Minnesota, I couldn't sleep at night before a game because I knew that if I didn't accept a challenge, a one-on-one fight, I'd call myself a chicken and I wouldn't be able to live with myself. So if we were playing Philadelphia or some other team with two or three tough guys, I had it in my mind that I was probably going to fight them. If it didn't happen, it didn't happen. But I knew that if I hit them, and I always followed my checks, it would happen because I had to stand up for my team. That meant the summers were so good because I didn't have to worry about who I was going to have to fight."

His religion, he says, gives him comfort. "God has always been in my life, but the last three or four years it's been stronger. I've always gone to church as long as the minister is good and can teach me things. But I don't push religion on anybody," he says. "It's up to them."

Thinking back to Prince Albert, where he grew up on a farm, he says, "One day, my father told me we were going to town and I was going to try out for a team. I think I was nine. I said I didn't want to go because they don't like country kids in town—they make fun of us. But he said we're going, so I went to the practice—and I made the team. We played on

Saturday night and I didn't even know what offside was, but I think I got four goals."

He adds that he couldn't even raise the puck. "So my father got me some pucks, and after I'd done my chores and my homework I'd practice shooting at the garage door and I'd shoot and shoot until it got so dark I couldn't see the door anymore. All through the years I always worked hardest at the things I was weak at. If I couldn't turn left, that's what I worked on. Another blessing is that my birthday is December 31. That meant that, the way hockey was set up, I was always playing with kids older than me, sometimes nearly two years older, so I had to work that much harder just to keep up. Later on, in tournaments, I'd be fourteen and find myself up against seventeen- and eighteen-year-olds."

After playing with the Swift Current Broncos in the WHL, Ruskowski joined the Houston Aeros of the old World Hockey Association. (His teammates included Gordie Howe and Howe's sons, Mark and Marty.)

"Houston drafted me in the second round and Chicago in the third," he says. "Billy Reay was the Blackhawks coach and he phoned me—in those days they phoned—and said we small guys had to stick together and all the rah-rah-rah. I was pretty happy because Chicago was my father's favorite team—but after all that stuff from Reay they didn't come up with much, and Houston offered me a three-year, no-cut contract."

Following four years with the Aeros and one with Winnipeg, also in the WHA, Ruskowski spent nine seasons in the NHL, split between Chicago, Los Angeles and Pittsburgh. His playing career ended with parts of two seasons in Minnesota.

"The Lord blessed me in many ways, but he knew and I knew that that was the end of my playing career," he says. "That last season, I played only three games. I got a goal and an assist, but Pierre Pagé had come in as coach and he wanted younger guys. I always tried to be positive in practice, though, right to the end. I didn't want to be a sulker or a pouter. If a guy had a good game, I'd go and tell him." He expects the same from his players. "I worked hard, I stuck up for my team and I stuck up for myself," he says. "That's what I look for."

He goes on, comparing a player he had last year to the late Keith Magnuson, a teammate with the Blackhawks, who, although just average in size, took an abnormal amount of punishment. "I loved the way this kid would stick in there, stick up for himself, for his teammates. And he was a pleasure to be around. Anyway, he decided to go back to school, to become a pharmacist, when he realized he wasn't going to get much further in hockey. He asked me what I thought, and I said that yeah, he'd made the right decision."

About the worst thing a player can do for any coach is to quit on him—on or off the ice. Ruskowski tells a story about a player who walked out on the team last year, two games before the playoffs were to begin, because he said Ruskowski was too hard on him. "And the father backed the kid up, wanted to know why I was picking on his son. Then the kid changes his mind, wants to come back, so I went to the players and said, 'Remember, he didn't just quit on me, he quit on you, too.' I put it to a vote and it was 'No,' 'No,' 'No,' and 'Hell, no!' Since then he's quit two other teams."

What he wants from his players, he says, is that "they play hard, win championships and move to higher leagues. As much as this is AA hockey and not as fast and skilled as the NHL, I think it's more exciting. There's more action, guys working hard—not just defense—a few scraps, fans getting into it. I go to an NHL game now and I don't see that at all. It's often boring, just boring."

He continues, really warming up. "They're trying [in the NHL] to make all these changes and they're not working. What I'd like is to see every rink Olympic-sized. I watch the Olympics and I think that's the finest hockey I've seen in a long time—guys skating, making passes. Right now, the guys being so big, they don't have room to make a play. I know it's expensive, but it would improve hockey so much. The NHL is short-sighted and it'll cost them in the long run."

But Ruskowski has his funny stories, too. The Winnipeg Jets of 1978–79, he says, were a team divided between the original Jets and players from the Houston Aeros, such as himself, who had joined them after Houston folded. During the season, the Jets traded for a goalie, Gary (Suitcase) Smith. "He came walking into the locker room and sat down," Ruskowski says. "He was pretty much overweight. He says, 'Half you guys don't know me, [but] I've been on around fifteen teams in the last two years. My goals-against average is about 5.33 and I've won one game and lost thirteen. But don't let that fool you—I'm not that good.' Everybody just cracked up. You could see we were coming together as a team."

After Ruskowski left Minnesota as a player, he coached for nine years, beginning back in his native Saskatchewan with the WHL's Saskatoon Blades in 1989. His last team before the Bucks was the Knoxville Speed of the United Hockey League, which used to be the Colonial Hockey League. Sandwiched in between there were two years with the Houston Aeros when they were in the IHL. That's where he met Glenn Hart, who became the Bucks' co-owner. When Hart bought into the Bucks, he asked Ruskowski to coach them. "Glenn Hart is a good man," Ruskowski says. "One of the best people I've ever met. I guess I'd do anything for him, so after praying, asking for guidance, I came here."

Joe Dominey, the radio broadcaster, is as intense as the coach. He says Ruskowski doesn't handle losing well. "And he won't tolerate anything but total effort. I guess that's the way he played."

This is Dominey's first year in Laredo. He broadcast minor-league baseball before switching to Seattle's team in the WHL. Last year, he was with the CHL's Memphis River Kings. "I really enjoy the flow of the sport, the contact, the speed and skill, and by far it's hardest to do on radio," he says. He calls it "a constant challenge," but he thinks "hands down, it is the best sport around. I just wish that I'd grown up with it."

Of his broadcast audience, he says "they have a hard time quantifying the ratings. Our geographic reach is more than a hundred miles into Mexico and all over south Texas."

Dominey might be described as hyperactive, which he likely has to be to handle his workload. Besides broadcasting all the games, he handles publicity and media relations not only for the Bucks, but for a fledgling arena football team, too. He collects stats and files copy to any outlet that wants it, such as the *Laredo Morning Times*, which doesn't send a hockey writer on the road. ("That ensures they won't carry something negative about us," he says, with about as close to a smile as he can muster.) If he's not on the phone in his cubicle, which seems too small for him, or chasing information on his computer or preparing broadcast notes or sending off press releases or printing them out, he's on his cell phone while he either races around the building with his clipboard or drives off somewhere in his modest white Nissan, which also looks too small for him.

Derek Craft, the equipment manager, also in his early thirties, is a little looser than Joe. "Losing on the road makes for long bus trips home," he says. "No cards, no movies. Just the game up on the video." He laughs. "And it's not even our fault, Joe's and mine."

Craft comes from Johnstown, in Pennsylvania. He played hockey in high school and for one semester in college until a serious (non-hockey) neck injury forced him to quit. He says he began to work for the hometown Jets—the model for the Charlestown Chiefs in the movie *Slap Shot*—because he loved hockey and wanted to stay in the game.

As equipment manager, he's probably closer to the players than anybody else is, including the coach or their wives and girlfriends, and he's seen a lot of them over the years. After Johnstown, he moved to the ECHL's Mobile Mystics and then to the Tallahassee Tiger Sharks, also in the East Coast league, where he doubled as equipment manager for Tallahassee's arena football team, the Thunder. He spent one season with the San Angelo Outlaws of the CHL, then came to Laredo last season, the Bucks' first.

"We've got a good blend of players here," he says. "They're okay, all of them."

"I guess it takes only two or three guys to really screw up a team," someone says to him.

Craft replies, "Two or three? "One can do it. It takes only one."

In minor professional hockey there are seven or eight leagues and nearly every one of the forty-nine continental U.S. states, from Alaska to Florida, has at least one pro team, not counting the NHL clubs. Then there are the dozens of teams in the United Kingdom and Europe. Among the Bucks' older players are Chris Grenville—the shooter Ruskowski mentioned, who comes from Thorold, near St. Catharines, and who played junior in Sault Ste. Marie—and Jef Bes, from Tillsonbourg, near Windsor.

The Bucks are Grenville's eighth pro team in eleven years. For Bes, who played his junior hockey in Hamilton and Guelph, the Bucks are his sixteenth. His résumé includes a season and a half in Finland and a stop in Germany. "I even played in Slovenia," Bes says. He thinks the top Finnish league is one of the best outside the NHL. "It's a fantastic league," he says. "And Germany, too. Lots of AHL players."

As for Laredo, he says, sitting up in the stands after practice, "Terry and I crossed paths about five years ago. I flew into Knoxville; I'd come back from Finland and I was kinda wavering about whether I was going to play anymore. It wasn't the right situation for me, but Terry was coaching there and I liked him and I liked the way he handled things. I really respected him."

Derek Clancy, Bes's coach last year in Jackson, Mississippi, of the ECHL, had played for Ruskowski and, Bes says, also learned to coach from him. "So I did a lot of research, spoke to a lot of people, and liked what I found," he says. "I just wanted to go to a place to win a championship, and that's what Terry's goal is. And the fans here are awesome. They get right into the game. They're like a sixth attacker. Last year in Jackson we were getting about 1,000 a game. It was a franchise struggling for money. It's tough to play in a situation like that. Here, we're getting around 6,000. It's exciting. And I like playing for Terry. He's demanding, but that's the way it should be. He's the first guy to tell you that you're doing well. He's also the first guy to kick you in the butt if you're not. He has the total support of the players. Just look at our won-lost record. That tells you."

In contrast to Grenville and Bes, twenty-one-year-old Mike Amodeo, a forward from Hamilton and a graduate of the Kitchener Rangers, is in his first year as a professional. A nice-looking, soft-spoken young man in glasses, who nevertheless takes a lot of penalties, Amodeo is the property of the Florida Panthers. He has rejoined the Bucks from Florida's AHL affiliate in San Antonio. He likes it in Laredo because he gets more ice time than he did with the Rampage, and he's confident that he'll be back up. In the meantime, unlike most of the others, he says unashamedly that he misses home. "I like being with my parents and my two sisters," he says. "This is the farthest I've been away. It's a big difference between here and home and the forty-five miles between Kitchener and home. I like playing for Terry, though. He's a good coach—really makes you want to win, and his door's always open. Anything bothering you, you can go right in."

Yesterday, the team traveled to Hidalgo—which, like Laredo, is on the Mexican border—to play the Rio Grande Valley Killer Bees. It's a three-hour trip. That's not bad—it's eleven hours to Amarillo and sixteen to New Mexico. Going to Indianapolis must seem like a trip to the moon. The Bucks' usual sleeper bus, which has berths for twelve (the players take turns), is being repaired. Instead, a standard seats-only bus waits for them at the Laredo arena. The players bring pillows and blankets aboard, which makes them look like kids heading over to a friend's house for a sleepover. They and Ruskowski travel in the team's dark-blue-and-yellow nylon tracksuits.

At exactly two-thirty, the bus pulls out. Right away, Bobby Chad Mitchell, the forward from Nipawin who loves life, lies down on the floor under the seats, stretches out across the aisle, and falls asleep, his head on his pillow. Anyone moving around at that end of the bus has to step over him. The other players also settle down, and there's barely a sound. Outside, the cold, wet weather exaggerates the meanness of the dreary gray-brown plain and stunted bush that reaches to the horizon. About halfway to Hildago the bus pulls in at an immigration checkpoint. The immigration officer sticks his head in the door, Ruskowski says something to him, and the officer smiles, wishes him good luck and waves the bus on.

U.S. immigration is particularly attentive to what happens along the Mexican border. Usually, there's no problem where a hockey team is concerned, but now and then they're stopped. One time, Ruskowski says, there was a Swede whose visa had run out or whose paperwork wasn't up to scratch. As the officials don't bother Canadians much, Ruskowski advised the player, if asked whether he was born in Canada—as most of the team was—not to speak, just to nod. "So the immigration guy asks him and instead of nodding the kid says"—and here Ruskowski puts on a passable Swedish accent—"'*Ja*, I am being born in Canada.' That sure held us up for a while."

The only other stop is for $150 worth of gas. When the bus is about half an hour from its destination, the players begin to stir. Through the windows, the forbidding countryside is looking more gentle and certainly more green now that they're deep into the fertile Rio Grande Valley, with all its farms. On the outskirts of Hidalgo, the Valley town that is home to the Bees, about thirty migrant workers in bright yellow rain ponchos are stooped over in a very wet, very green field. No one on the bus seems to know what they're picking. Beans, someone at the back says. Someone else says no, not beans. They all agree, though, given the rotten weather, that no matter what they're picking, it's a shitty job.

When the bus reaches Hidalgo and the Dodge Arena, which is named for the car, Derek Craft, the players and a couple of other Bucks staff members unload the equipment and carry it through the back door to their dressing rooms. Joe Dominey, with all his broadcasting gear slung over his shoulder, looks like he could use a Dodge himself. Inside, he asks one of the arena employees if the game is going to start on time. The man says it should. Dominey walks on, heading for the press box. "They hardly ever start on time here—hardly ever," he says. "There's always something. Ten or fifteen minutes late—always something."

Ruskowski stays behind on the bus to exchange his nylon tracksuit for a dark blue business suit, white shirt and tie.

A little later, in the seats behind the Plexiglas at the end of the rink where the Zamboni and the players enter and exit, a Laredo Buck, Steve Simoes, sits alone in his black hockey underwear and begins to tape three sticks. It's about ninety minutes to game time. Simoes, a forward, is twenty-five. He's a polite, purposeful young man who says he likes to do this when the team is on the road because it helps him get a feel for the rink, even if he's played in it before. "Every rink is different," he says. "This is a good one. In Corpus Christi, the boards are uneven; pucks takes crazy bounces. It's a small building. Austin is a big building, but dim. Amarillo has a small ice surface."

This is Simoes' first year with the Bucks. He was born in Brossard, on the outskirts of Montreal. He played two years in the Quebec Major Junior Hockey League, sat out a year to satisfy Canadian intercollegiate rules, and then played three years with the University of Ottawa, where he got a degree in economics. His parents had emigrated from Portugal, and he speaks four languages: English, French, Portuguese and Spanish—a nice thing when you find yourself living on the Mexican border. He said he'd hoped to catch on this season with the Ottawa Senators' AHL affiliate in Binghamton, but instead he ended up down here. He's prepared to play for another six or seven years, as long as he's enjoying it. "I'll just have to see," he says. "It's hard to get an NHL contract coming out of the CIAU [the Canadian university system] compared with if you played your university hockey in the States."

Another Buck who played in college is Mark Matier, a defenseman who, like his teammate Chris Grenville, hails from Thorold, Ontario. Originally a Washington Capitals draft pick, he's been around. After three seasons with the Sault Ste. Marie Greyhounds in the OHL, where he was part of the 1993 team that won the Memorial Cup, he spent a year in the AHL and another in what's now the United Hockey League. Then he decided to go to university because, although he wasn't sure how long he would play professional hockey, he was sure that he needed more education. He chose St. Francis Xavier, in Antigonish, Nova Scotia, after getting a call from the St. FX coach, Danny Flynn, who'd been an assistant coach in the Soo. "We'd been friends since then," Matier says. "He was a helluva coach."

The eligibility rules are the same whether a player is leaving the pros or major junior to play university hockey. This means that, like Simoes, Matier had to sit out a year. There's no such restriction against playing amateur, though, so he joined the nearby Truro Bearcats and went with them to the Allan Cup playdowns. But the next season, when the Bearcats won the Cup, Matier was playing his first of three seasons for Danny Flynn. Then came four years in the United Kingdom before joining Laredo last fall.

Matier is twenty-nine and is proud of his Memorial Cup, but he knows the level of hockey he's at now, that step below the AHL, is as high as he'll climb.

"The NHL is the elite, and I thought once that I might have a chance to play there, but it wasn't my ultimate goal," he says. "I just play hockey because it's fun. And I love it here. The fans are great and the hockey's a lot better than I thought. We have a good team and hopefully we can win the championship." He says that in university hockey the top couple of lines were as good as in the CHL, but the college teams didn't have the same depth. "Here we have four lines and three defense—more depth," he says. "You don't get that at school."

After professional hockey, Matier would like to teach school. He and his wife have two boys. They met in the Soo. "I hope I can teach there or in Thorold," he says. "It'd be nice for the kids to be around their grandparents."

The press box in the Dodge Arena is small and can get crowded. There are chairs for about five or six people. Joe Dominey gets right to work, setting up his broadcasting equipment against an end wall so that, if he's going to be bothered, at least it can be only from one side. He is on his own and is surrounded by so much stuff—wires, cable, plugs, headsets, mikes, black boxes—that he looks like his own electronics exhibition. A couple of other reporters are there, including a young blonde woman who covers hockey for the McAllen *Monitor*, a local newspaper. Her name is Kristin Huber. She's from Minnesota, loves hockey, but had to come all the way to the Rio Grande Valley to get a job covering it. "There was nothing at home," she says. "Nothing for me in Minnesota."

It's after 7 o'clock. Dominey looks over at the clock that counts down to the time the game is meant to start. "See?" he says. "They're putting more time on the clock. Ten minutes. We'll be at least ten minutes late starting. Jesus."

The arena is smaller than the Laredo Center but is just as neat and comfortable. This is the Killer Bees' first year. "A lot of markets peak in that first year, but we have only 5,500 seats, so people can keep coming," says Trey Medlock. He is the Bees GM and president; he is tall, middle-aged, smartly dressed and cheerful. He's standing in the press box, smiling down approvingly at all the seats that he knows will soon be filled. "There are two and a half million people in the Rio Grande Valley," he says. "It's taken a bit of educating [about hockey], but we're happy. We're only going to grow. This game has been sold out since Monday, and there's a good chance we'll sell out our last eight [home] games."

A couple of minutes later, in comes Len Buckborough, a native of Niagara Falls, who's also a Bees promoter. He says that he picked the Rio Grande Valley for winter retirement after visiting here. "It beats Florida," he says. His business card identifies him as the Winter Texan Coordinator. "Winter Texans" is the term used here for Canadian snowbirds. "I'm the liaison between the Canadians here and the hockey team," Buckborough says. He says there are 500 trailer parks, with lots of Canadians in them, over the 100-mile stretch of the Rio Grande Valley between Rio Grande City and Brownsville.

"Five hundred?"

"Five hundred."

He and Medlock are confident that these Winter Texans will show up for the games.

Buckborough is reminded of the remark attributed to Toronto-born Jack Kent Cooke when he owned the NHL's Los Angeles Kings. Attendance was down and Cooke reportedly said that he knew why: he'd figured out that the estimated 350,000 Canadians living in the Los Angeles area had all moved there because they hated hockey. Buckborough shrugs. "I don't think that'll happen here," he says.

At this game, one Edmonton Oilers and one or two Toronto Maple Leafs sweaters are spotted. Most of the crowd seems to be Hispanic, and any other hockey sweaters bear the crest of the Killer Bees.

Another young local reporter says that the trend in minor league hockey is towards smaller arenas, built to hold 5,000 or so. "They pack this place and the atmosphere is great," he says. "It's good for the fans and the players. You go to a big rink, like Oklahoma City, and it's a third full and it's depressing for everybody, like being in a tomb. Our rink is perfect for the minors."

There's no tomb here. The young man has to shout to be heard over the ear-splitting pregame music, the sound effects accompanying the animation on the Jumbotron and the non-stop yelling of the PA announcer—"Get your tickets now for the *KILLER BEEEEEES'* next game! Let's hear it for the *KILLER BEEEEEES!*"

"People complain [about the noise], but they never do anything about it," says Kristin Huber, the Minnesota native, who has to shout to be heard.

The referee is Steve Cruickshank. He's from Brantford, Ontario. He stops by the press box for a chat and a pregame doughnut from the food tray. "Don't tell anybody," he says, grinning and biting into one. Then he says, "I like it here, this league, and anyway, I'm thirty-six, a little long in the tooth to move up. Besides, like most jobs, you'd have to put up with the politics and the backstabbing." He looks out at the lights over the ice. "This is about as a bright as I want it to be for me."

The Bees coach is Tracy Egeland; he's from Lethbridge, Alberta. At thirty-three he's the youngest in the league. Before getting to the CHL as an assistant with Lubbock, he played twelve years in the high minors—the IHL and the AHL. His Bees roster lists eleven Canadians, six Americans and a Slovenian. They'll all be on the ice tonight, giving them sixteen skaters. The Bucks are going with fourteen, which means only five on defense. However, they hold a wide winning margin over the Bees so far this season and are more than 30 points ahead of them in the Southeast Division of the Southern Conference. A Bees fan, sipping a beer, says, "Getting this league straight—north, south, divisions, conferences, all that—should help your geography." But in this game, things don't go right, almost from the start—from the moment Joe Dominey, over the constant din of the crowd, introduces the game to his listeners as "The Border Town Battle."

Although the Bucks are badly outplayed and take a handful of what seem like foolish penalties, the Killer Bees can't score on David Guerra until late in the third period. When regulation time ends, the Bees have outshot the Bucks 47–20, but the score is tied 1–1. Only Guerra, born in St. Léonard, Quebec, who played in the Saskatchewan junior league with the Estevan Bruins and later with Michigan's Wayne State University, has kept the Bucks in the game. Five minutes of four-on-four overtime settles nothing. A shoot-out does, though: the first three of the five selected Bees shooters score, while the first three Bucks don't. The game goes into the record book as a 2–1 Bees victory.

After the game the players shower and dress quickly. It's not as if they're going to want to hang around the dressing room congratulating themselves. They know they've played badly, and there's barely a sound as they board the bus. A few minutes along, on the edge of Hidalgo, the driver, with Ruskowski's okay, pulls into a truck stop. The players want to pick up something to supplement the sandwiches and bottled water that were waiting for them on the bus.

Ruskowski, back in his tracksuit, is sitting in the front seat, the one just inside the door. "You've got three minutes," he says as three players file off and trot through the rain to the store. He's obviously upset by tonight's play. Two more players follow. "You've got two minutes," he tells them. Then he says to three more, "You've got thirty seconds."

After a couple more minutes, when the bus is on its way, Ruskowski collects the videotape of the game from Dominey, who is sitting a couple of seats behind him, and puts it on. There's a monitor at the front of the bus, but there's no sound, only the pictures. In the dark, it's hard to see who is watching the game besides Ruskowski. When the tape gets to point where the Bees score the tying goal, Ruskowski stops and replays it five times.

The bus gets back to the Laredo Center at two-thirty in the morning. The players head straight for their cars and SUVs, but Derek Craft, the equipment manager, has to get everything in order for the next day. He doesn't finish his work until about five; his day had started at seven-thirty the morning before.

The next day, after the morning skate that lasted from eleven until noon, Ruskowski is in his office. He's much more relaxed than he was after last night's game. He says the Bees forechecked the Bucks hard. "And we're not a team that likes to dump the puck in," he says. "We like to make plays, and their defense was standing us up pretty well."

Right now he's working on getting a player or two from up in Michigan, from the OHL's Saginaw Spirit, to reinforce a lineup depleted by call-ups to the AHL and injuries. Moe Mantha, a friend of Ruskowski's since they were teammates in Pittsburgh, coaches Saginaw. "They're not going to make the playoffs," Ruskowski says, "and he's got this big center. I phoned him about him."

Another player, this one sent down to Laredo from San Antonio, may be slow getting into the lineup because his visa has expired and he has to reapply to get into the United States.

A player Ruskowski is definitely after for next year is Aaron Starr, a rangy center from the Manitoba junior team, the Opaskwayak Cree Nation Blizzard. "I've already talked with Glen Watson [the coach]," he says. "We'll have to see."

Tonight's return game against the Bees will be the Bucks' third in four days. The first of the three—the Wednesday before the Friday game in Hidalgo—was an 11 a.m. game especially for schoolchildren. The teachers called it a "field trip." The parking lot was filled with scores of yellow school buses and the stands were crammed with screaming kids. It doesn't matter whether it's southern Texas or Rimouski, Thunder Bay or Viking, Alberta, the yellow buses are the same. The kids are, too.

The noise was relentless and earsplitting. But whether it was inspired by the holiday from school or the thrill of the game was hard to say. However, local youngsters are getting to know the game. For one thing, the Laredo Arena has free public skating for them on certain days, and the skates are there waiting, racks of them—just a matter of getting the right size. Then it's off to the ice, more often than not on their ankles, yelling at each other, mostly in Spanish. Wow, right where the pros play! And sometimes a couple of the Bucks are there to show them the way.

The Bucks beat the Fort Worth Brahmas, 6–3, in the game for the kids to clinch the CHL's Southern Conference title. After it was over, the Bucks Booster Club had a meal ready for both teams—in separate rooms. Max Birbraer, the Israeli, a tall, fair, twenty-three year-old who now lives in Aurora, outside Toronto, ate with his girlfriend. Birbraer is a center and is one of the team's best skaters. The New Jersey Devils drafted him, and he played three exhibition games with them last fall, so he's a bit discouraged to be down here after getting so close to an NHL job.

He was born in Ust-Kamenogorsk, an industrial city of 350,000 in Kazakhstan. "Basically, it's like Laredo," he says. "All they have is a hockey team." He began playing when he was six, and that was where he learned to skate. "That's all there was to do," he says. "Hours at a time." He remembers when his teams didn't have enough sticks to go around and players coming off the ice would have to give their sticks to the players coming on. But he had a great coach, he says: Boris Alexandrov, one of the Soviet stars of the 1976 Canada Cup. (Alexandrov was killed in a car accident in July 2002.) The captain of Birbraer's team his final season was Nik Antropov. When he was fifteen, his parents emigrated to Israel.

"Who would know that three days later I was on the ice there and after skating for fifteen minutes, just in jeans—I didn't have my equipment—I was asked to play on the Israeli national team."

What followed was another move, this time to Canada and junior A, first in Shelburne, Ontario, and then for two years in Newmarket. "I got 50 goals in 47 games there," Birbraer says. He was drafted by the New Jersey Devils. Next came a return trip to Israel to see his family, where he was promptly jailed because he hadn't done his national service.

"I was in jail a month and then three months in the army," he says, "but I was riding so high [because of hockey] I was just having fun."

When he returned to North America he played three years for the Devils' AHL affiliate, the Albany River Rats. Then he signed with Florida and was sent to their AHL team, the San Antonio Rampage, who assigned him to Laredo.

"It was hard going from such a high, playing for the Devils, to such a low," he says. "But then I thought I may as well have some fun here, because there are some things you can't control. And I've always played as hard as I can."

Birbraer says his greatest supporter is his grandfather back in Kazakhstan. "I call him, and he always cries when things don't work out for me," he says. "But I went back for the first time in seven years, and we agreed that as long as I did my best, that's all I could do."

Right now, Max is content; his girlfriend is down from New York to visit him for a week. She settles in right behind the glass with members of the Bucks Booster Club in their caps and T-shirts.

It's almost game time, and outside the guys are beginning to clean up and pack away their grill. Inside, through doors that carry large warnings (in both Spanish and English) that it's against the law to bring in a concealed firearm—there's no smoking, either—the spotless arena seems almost to glow. Hundreds of youngsters are in the mainly Hispanic crowd. Young and old meander along the concourses—expansive enough, if they were roads, for three or four cars to drive abreast—buying tacos, nachos, ice cream, fruit juice, fresh fruit, cotton candy, soda pop and beer. Pucks bearing the Bucks crest are moving at $10 apiece and so are little souvenir hockey sticks and T-shirts with the Bucks logo. Hockey sweaters are moving, too, but not as quickly. They start at $55 a crack, and that's for the kids' sizes.

Jim Hayhurst came out of early retirement to take a job as a maintenance man when the Laredo Center opened. He's on a break now, just standing and watching the crowd. "Hockey fans seem pretty down to earth. I can't think of any real trouble since I've been here," he says. "Security has probably had to kick out only one or two guys at most. And I'm starting to like it, to like hockey. I'd never seen a game until I came here."

After a moment he adds something that the Chamber of Commerce and the Tourist Bureau likely would rather he hadn't. "Let's face it," he says, "there isn't much else to do here. We got, what? Three theaters? Yeah, three theaters and a bowling alley. That's about it."

The fans are settling in now. The PA announcer tells them, in Spanish and English, that "This is family entertainment. Profanity will not be tolerated." He also warns against throwing anything on the ice—"except hats after a hat trick." Anything else, he says, "and you'll be gone."

When the game gets going, the Bucks hold a wide margin of play, but it takes another shoot-out before they win, 5–4. A fat man in his forties, wearing his Laredo Bucks cap backwards, jumps from his seat, shouting (in English, but with a heavy Spanish accent), "We wins! We wins! We good! We good!"

Win or lose, Terry Ruskowski likes shoot-outs. "I don't want to leave a game that ends in a tie," he says. "Nobody should pay good money to see a tie. We have shoot-outs here, and the crowd loves them—you should hear them when the announcer says, 'Number sixteen, Chris Grenville, is going to shoot,' and then when he scores . . . Even if we lose, we get a point anyway."

Early the next morning, when the sun is barely up, Max Birbraer and his girlfriend are at the Laredo Airport. Max is dead tired from last night's game. But he's not there to see his girlfriend off—she's the one saying goodbye to him. He has his hockey sticks with him and he's catching the 6:30 flight to Dallas en route to San Antonio. He was still in the dressing room when he got word that Florida had promoted him to the AHL's San Antonio Rampage. "They have some injuries, I guess," he says. "I don't know how long I'll be up. In this game, you never know."

On April 28, 2004, the Bucks defeated the Bossier-Shreveport Mudbugs 3–2 in overtime of game seven to win the CHL's President's Cup. It was Terry Ruskowski's first championship as a coach. Aaron Starr, the Aboriginal from Saskatoon, who won the Manitoba junior league scoring title with the OCN Blizzard, joined Laredo after the Blizzard were knocked out of their playoffs. "We're really proud of him," said Wayne Hawrysh, a Blizzard assistant coach. "Aaron was very close to us, kind of adopted." Max Birbraer was with San Antonio for four days, then finished the season back in Laredo.

CHAPTER 6

The Spartans

EAST LANSING, MICHIGAN • A U.S. immigration officer at Port Huron, the border crossing on the Michigan side of the St. Clair River, across from Sarnia, Ontario, says, "If you're going to Michigan State, tell Ron Mason hello for me." It seems nearly everyone knows Ron Mason. He's the athletic director at Michigan State University in East Lansing, but before that, he coached Michigan State's hockey team for years. "Tell him it's the guy at the border who always kids him about his green truck," the immigration officer says. "And have a nice day."

That evening, hundreds of people stream into the Breslin Center on the Michigan State campus. They have the hottest ticket in town right now. Dozens of others, without tickets, are milling around outside. Most are students, and they're trying to knock scalpers down from their nearly $100 price tag. "He still wants $85," one young man says to another. "Screw him. I can't go that high." They still stand there, though, in the mild March evening, hands in windbreaker pockets, checking out the scene; but, with time running out, so are the tickets, and so are their hopes. Finally, the two young men look at each other, shrug their shoulders and head off into the deepening dusk to watch the game on TV at a bar.

Tonight, it's not hockey—that's in a couple of days. It's basketball: the MSU Spartans against the University of Wisconsin Badgers. An MSU victory will give the Spartans at least a share of the Big Ten championship, which would be quite something given their 5–7 start, but it's what the huge crowd expects. Besides, this is the Breslin, where the home team has won 95 percent of its Big Ten games since 1997–98.

The crowd has swelled to more than 19,000—students, graduate students, alumni, friends of MSU. There isn't an empty seat. And because it's a long way from Madison, Wisconsin, to East Lansing, it's mainly an MSU crowd.

"There's no doubt that hockey ranks behind basketball and football here, the same as at any Big Ten school," says Ron Mason, the athletic director with the green truck. "But our hockey fans are just as passionate about their game as our football and basketball fans. This is real hockey country, and it always has been."

Back inside the Breslin, many of the basketball crowd are clad in MSU's distinctive forest green—sweaters or shirts or windbreakers with the little white Spartan insignia on the collar or breast. Some of the younger ones have painted their faces green. They're loud, energetic and good-natured. Michigan State's swinging brass band includes eight tubas and, if not seventy-six trombones, then at least a couple of rows of them. When the band is not giving a spirited imitation of Basie or Goodman, the audio system is cranked up and the place is rockin' and shakin' to the sounds of Jerry Lee Lewis or James Brown.

The symbol of MSU sports, the eleven-foot-high, three-ton statue of a Spartan, which stands near the athletic sites, is represented by the mascot, Sparty. In his fiberglass mask and vinyl warrior breastplate, Sparty isn't quite as tall as the statue, but he's still a good seven feet. He's a comic book creation, bounding about with his fixed, heavy-browed frown, joining the fifty or so cheerleaders—boys and girls—who ring the floor, in exhorting everybody to get with it.

It's like a giant party. And although it's a school night, quite a few kids in the ten-to-twelve-year-old range are there with their parents, giving the place a friendly, family feel, almost a Disney-movie quality. But this crowd is intense, too. Looking around, it's hard to imagine that many of them bought their tickets and came in just for the hell of it or because there isn't much on TV tonight; they want their team to win in the worst way.

Towards the end of the first half it's pretty close, the teams exchanging two- and three-point advantages. Peter Johnson, who graduated in engineering from MSU in the late sixties, made the ninety-minute drive to the game from his home in Detroit. That's where he grew up, watching the Red Wings of Gordie Howe and Ted Lindsay, Terry Sawchuk, Alex Delvecchio and Bill Gadsby. He tries to get here as often as possible for football, basketball or hockey, and although tonight's game is basketball, he says, "This is what hockey used to be like when I was a kid and you could get close to the players, really see them." He's talking about the courtside fans here, who could probably reach out and touch the athletes. "Now you got face masks and visors and helmets so they all look the same, and all that Plexiglas running around the whole rink, sealing them off. You might as well be watching a pinball game. In basketball, you're still part of it. You can see and feel and hear almost everything, even from up here. You can the see the sweat, for God's sake—hear them breathing."

It's not a good night for the Spartans, though. Perhaps they didn't sweat enough. They blow a 3-point lead in the final minutes and lose 68–64 in overtime. The crowd is stunned, collectively shaking its head as it exits—disbelieving, sorry and sad.

The next day's *Lansing State Journal* has six stories on the front page of its sports section. One of them, at the bottom, deals with baseball's Barry Bonds and steroids. Another, also below the fold, is on the possibility of MSU playing a basketball game next season on the deck of an aircraft carrier. The other four are about last night's game. Under the headline "Devastating Defeat," the reporters accuse the Spartans of choking, letting "the chance at crown slip away." It turns out a championship banner had been set up in the rafters above the court, ready to be unfurled at the final buzzer. "And that's where it stayed as MSU basketball came unraveled at the worst possible time." (The basketball team didn't know the banner was there; the coach said that if he had, he would have ordered it removed.) The newspaper also reported that some of the players were crying so much, they couldn't even talk to reporters, another good example of how seriously they take their basketball, not to mention their football, here.

But, according to one of the hockey team's assistant coaches, hockey isn't that far behind. "The hockey program has been so successful and brought the university so much respect that you certainly don't feel like a second-class citizen," says Tommy Newton, a native of Uxbridge, Ontario, and a one-time Oshawa General. "You feel like part of the group, and to the credit of the other coaches, they make you feel like part of the group."

The Munn Arena, where they play hockey, is next door to the Breslin Center. It's named after the late Clarence "Biggie" Munn, who was not a hockey man but the longtime MSU football coach.

The Munn was opened in 1974. It looks like many thirty-year-old arenas in small-town Canada—that is, it has the standard 200-by-85-foot ice surface and the ice is good, there is hardly a bad seat in the place, and it smells vaguely of mildew. But although it's beginning to show its age, the dressing rooms, offices and private boxes recently got a $4-million face-lift; in other words, it's a fine rink.

"We have a capacity of around 6,500 and we've been full for 328 games in a row," Ron Mason says. This means, as MSU's hockey people like to point out, that there hasn't been an empty seat since December 1985, a streak that began with a sold-out game against Northern Michigan.

A native of Blyth, in western Ontario near Lake Huron, the stocky, sixty-four-year-old Mason is friendly and cheerful, but he's also busy and businesslike, always on the go, which is hardly surprising seeing that he oversees a $54-million budget that covers twenty-five sports (men's and women's) in a school with 44,000—almost as many as the number of people who live in Cornwall, Ontario, or Fredericton, New Brunswick.

Looking dapper in a black sports shirt and black jacket that set off his thick white hair and full white mustache, Mason could be a leading man from a forties or fifties movie—a white-haired Brian Donlevy. He calls himself a "hockey junkie." Although he remains a Canadian citizen, Mason has been in the United States for more than forty years. After playing hockey at St. Lawrence University in upstate New York, he began his coaching career at Lake Superior State (in Sault Ste. Marie, Michigan) and then he went to Bowling Green (Ohio) before beginning his twenty-six years at MSU. When he stopped coaching two years ago to become MSU's athletic director, his overall record was 924–380–83, the best so far in college hockey history.

MSU plays football and basketball in a conference called the Big Ten, competing with such high-profile sports schools as Illinois, Wisconsin, the University of Michigan, Minnesota and Penn State. In hockey, the Spartans play in the twelve-team Central Collegiate Hockey Association (CCHA), which includes its historical and bitter rival, the University of Michigan (in Ann Arbor, near Detroit), as well as Notre Dame, Ohio State and Lake Superior State. Once a year, MSU goes all the way to Fairbanks to play the University of Alaska.

"One of the things is that the visibility that these sports [football, basketball and hockey] have often overshadows other aspects of a great university, and that's where it's out of whack a little bit," Mason says. "But that's the public [perception]; we can't control that. We don't get money from the university— we generate our own. I know it's hard for a professor to see a coach make millions of dollars [Mason says he's not talking about hockey coaches here], but that's what the market demands. As a general rule, things are run pretty well. I think we have respect for academics. A kid has to be working towards a degree to stay eligible for hockey. He can't just be taking a bunch of [easy] classes." (For example, Steve Swistak, a forward from West Bloomfield, Michigan, is going into medicine; Kevin Estrada, from Surrey, British Columbia, is majoring in kinesiology and psychology.)

On the walls of Mason's office are his two degrees in education—a BA from St. Lawrence and a master's from Pittsburgh—and some honorary degrees and diplomas. There are also several photos of him with sports celebrities—one with Don Shula, the famed coach of the Miami Dolphins of the National Football League; another with Grambling's great coach, Eddie Robinson; and still another with Joe Paterno, who's been the football coach at Penn State since as far back as most people can count. And there's one of him with Scotty Bowman, in which hockey's two winningest coaches are both grinning.

"I'm here setting the record for the most college wins, and at the same time Scotty's just down the road in Detroit with the Red Wings, setting it for the NHL," Mason says, pleased and proud of what he calls "quite a coincidence."

Mason, like Bowman, says he never saw himself as a players' coach. "I've always seen a players' coach as one who identifies more with the players than with the coaching," Mason says. "I tried to keep my presence as coach separate, and probably didn't socialize much with the players or hang around them all that much. And when I made decisions it was in the best interest of the team and the best interest of the program. To me, if you're the coach you better identify with the coach. That doesn't mean that I didn't care for them. I did everything in my power to help them do what they needed, but I didn't need them to like me. I stuck to my guns when it came to giving the team the best chance to win."

Something he learned more than fifty years ago from a coach in either bantam or peewee has stayed with him ever since. "The coach's name was Johnny James. His system was: first guy on the puck; second guy backs him up; third guy in the slot, and then there are the defensemen. I said to myself, 'That's a triangle and rectangle.' I've used that system forever. So I learned from one of my first coaches that there is a system to the game."

Not long ago, a team from a large Canadian university—say, Toronto, McGill or the University of Montreal—would easily handle MSU or another American school; but not anymore. For example, in exhibition games over the last several years MSU has beaten Western Ontario 5–0 and 6–0, Guelph 11–1 and Queen's 14–1. This season, the Spartans beat York, the Ontario university champions, 6–2. And they're doing it with Americans. A generation ago, U.S. college teams were laced with Canadians. This season, on MSU's twenty-five-man roster there are only five Canadians. And MSU's arch rival, the University of Michigan, has just three Canadians. The last time Michigan played the University of Toronto, in 1997, Michigan won 9–2.

According to Mason, a major reason for this success is the 1980 Olympic gold medal won by the Americans' Miracle on Ice team. "They were college kids who won that," Mason says. "Like the kids here, that's what they were—college kids."

Tom Newton agrees. "And Wayne Gretzky's trade to Los Angeles, too," he adds. "That made a big difference. He went to a nontraditional hockey area. And with the emergence of in-line skates it became a game in those nontraditional areas; suddenly you're seeing kids everywhere carrying hockey bags, playing ball hockey in parking lots, and you have players coming out of California, Florida, players coming out of Arizona. Now, suddenly, it's not the provincial game it once was. Michigan hasn't changed much. It's always been popular here."

Then there is the National Team Development Program. It's eight years old and takes what it considers the forty best teenage players in the U.S. and brings them to Ann Arbor, near Detroit, the home of the University of Michigan. There, they board with a family, go to school and play hockey at the Ann Arbor Ice Cube, with its three sheets of ice of different dimensions plus a million-dollar facility that includes locker rooms, a weight room and another training room. Recently, the teams have played in tournaments in Finland, Switzerland, Slovakia and Belarus. Three of its graduates are with MSU.

"That program was an outgrowth of USA Hockey's desire to compete at the world level," Newton says. "They hadn't had much success at the world juniors and they hadn't had a lot of success at world championships. They thought that if they took forty of their best players and brought them to one site as sixteen- and seventeen-year-olds, it would start to form a team and a philosophy of play that would lead to better performances. And with them winning a gold medal at the world juniors this year, I think it's proven that maybe it works. Players come from everywhere now."

Hockey was first played on the East Lansing campus in 1906, on the Red Cedar River. In 1921 it became a varsity sport when the players moved from the river to the outdoor tennis courts, which were flooded in an attempt to give hockey at least a fighting chance against the vagaries of weather. It didn't work. Photographs of Spartan hockey teams line the hallway that leads to the hockey offices and the team's quarters—a room for study, a press lounge, a weight and workout room, an equipment room and the dressing rooms. Under each photo is the team's record. Bad hockey weather cut the 1921 schedule play to only three games (it lost them all). Two years later the team didn't lose a game—it tied the only one it played. Then there's the 1931 team. The photograph shows nine men, all dressed in their equipment. They're holding their sticks and glowering into the camera, looking fed up and angry enough to take on the photographer. No wonder. Underneath that the picture is the notation, "All games cancelled because of bad weather."

For nearly twenty years after that last, aborted season, hockey was finished as an MSU sport, beaten by the weather. It wasn't until 1950, when artificial ice was installed in what is called the Demonstration Hall—a huge red-brick building that looks like an armory—that hockey made its comeback. Demo Hall stands out not only because of its size but because it's a bit shabby, inside and out. There is no longer any ice, even during hockey season, but the rink's boards are still up and so are the galleries that held the spectators. The high walls, with their white paint flaking off them, are of thick cement. All this, when the building is empty, gives it a cavernous—and sad and ghostly—air. It is used now by the university's Military Science department for ROTC drills and band practice. This afternoon, some schoolgirls are playing soccer indoors because it's too cold and wet outside. Those high cement walls amplify the slightest sound, the echoes piling up on each other. It's not hard to imagine what the noise must have been like during the twenty-five years that NCAA hockey was played here, before the Munn was opened. "Believe me, it was something," says one dad, here to collect his daughter. "I came here as a kid, and I don't think I've heard anything as consistently loud since."

Mason, who became MSU's coach in 1979, five years after the Munn was opened, grew up playing hockey in the Montreal Canadiens system. "When I was only fifteen, I played five games with an old Kitchener [senior] team run by Montreal. Willie O'Ree [the first black man to play in the NHL] was one of my linemates. I didn't think I was very good, but I must have been because I was with some pretty good players. But mind you, back then everyone was better than me. Montreal had Bobby Rousseau in their system, and Ralph Backstrom."

Mason was on the first Peterborough Petes Junior A team, put together in 1956 and affiliated with the Canadiens. He was sixteen. His coach was Baldy MacKay, a former Canadien. (Sam Pollock, who was later the Montreal GM, and Bowman coached the Petes, too, but Mason was gone by then.)

The next year, the Canadiens moved Mason to their Ottawa-Hull junior team. "We played an exhibition game against the Canadiens. We switched a couple of lines and I ended up with Maurice Richard, Jean Beliveau, Jacques Plante—all the guys I idolized," he says. "They were all so nice. And I still remember Doug Harvey saying, 'You're a center? Okay, on the breakout you come back and cut through the middle and that's where I'll hit you.' I went back, cut through the middle, and the puck was right on my stick."

It was about then, Mason says, that his mother laid down the law. "I'd taken some Grade 13 courses in Peterborough the year before, but except for math, which just came to me and I never had to study for, I just couldn't pass because of all the hockey. The next year, playing for the Ottawa-Hull Canadiens, I moved and I'm in Grade 13 at Glebe Collegiate in Ottawa and I'm flunking out. So at Christmas my mother tells Sam [coach Sam Pollock] that that's it, and she brings me home. I played Junior B in Seaforth and senior in Woodstock. But with Sam and Baldy, you learned how to win. I'll tell you, if you were in the Montreal organization at that time, losing wasn't accepted. I remember as a kid in Seaforth we'd been playing in a field, and the other kids would go home and I'd stay another two hours stickhandling around a stump, so maybe I'd always had that will to win."

The season after his mother yanked him from Ottawa, Mason was off to St. Lawrence. "My playing career was over when I went to college," he says. "College hockey wasn't what it is now. Our best players were just as good, but we didn't have the depth, and the coaching is much better today."

Like most hockey people, Mason is looking for ways to improve the game. "In hockey today, it's not the number of goals in a game that we should be looking at; what we want is more scoring chances," he says. "You used to watch a game, and it'd be great to see [Turk] Broda or Glenn Hall or Gump Worsley make these wonderful saves; but today, if there's more than fifteen scoring chances in a game a coach gets mad. I want to see a hundred scoring chances. We have to sell this game to the American public. You go to a college game [where they don't employ the red line at center] and it's pretty good, up and down. Then you go to an NHL game and there's nothing much happening. The NHL should take out the red line except for icing, allow the long passes, open up the game, get the players skating and get the puck around the net. That's where things happen."

He goes on: "I'd just like to see the game become more offensive than the way I coached it. There's no room. The kids take it away and the coaches coach it away. I don't think making the rink any bigger would help, because you'd be farther away from the net and there'd be less infighting and fewer scoring chances. The Europeans are a little better at the bigger ice surface than we are because they've had it their whole lives, but just making the rink bigger is not the answer."

Mason loves to talk about hockey. "Hockey's got everything you want in a game—speed, finesse, toughness—but its personality is gone," he says, leaning forward to emphasize his point, the same one made by the MSU alum two nights ago at the basketball game. "It went when the face mask, particularly the college full face mask, came in. Sure, it's cut down on eye injuries and lost teeth, and you'd never have it any other way, but back then you could see faces, eyes, expressions. Sometimes when I was coaching I'd have three scrimmages—the North American scrimmage, where you hit everything that moves; the European scrimmage, which was flow and go; then I'd give an old-time scrimmage: no helmets. The whole game changed. You'd see their eyes, their personalities. That's what we're missing, but I know we can't go back."

A couple of minutes' walk from Ron Mason's office is the 75,000-seat Spartan Stadium, where football is played. This is the stadium that was filled for the October 2001 outdoor hockey game in which MSU and the University of Michigan tied 3–3. It was the first outdoor game of its kind, two years before the NHL played its game in Edmonton's Commonwealth Stadium.

In between basketball's Breslin Center and the stadium is the Munn Arena, where the man who succeeded Mason as coach,

Rick Comley, and his assistant coaches, including Tom Newton, the former Oshawa General, are working the Spartans hard. For ninety minutes they practice rushes, two-on-two's, two-on-one's and power plays. Then the nets are moved and they play two-on-two on a narrow strip across the rink, using a lot of body in the much tighter space.

Tomorrow night, Friday, the Spartans begin a two-game home-and-home series against Michigan. Game one is to be played here and game two, the next night, is at the Joe Louis Arena in Detroit. Prior to tonight's game, Michigan and MSU have played each other 245 times dating back to 1922. Michigan has won 125 games to the Spartans' 110. Right now, Michigan is rated sixth in the country and MSU fourteenth. They've split the two games they've played already this season, each winning by the same score, 2–0.

For both sides, there's barely a rivalry to match it. It's college hockey's answer to college football's Army–Navy Game, to boxing's Rocky Graziano and Tony Zale or Ali–Frazier, tennis's Steffi Graf and Monica Seles. It's a rivalry the way it was when the Canadiens regularly played the Maple Leafs, before the NHL's expansion watered down all the glorious traditional rivalries.

Michigan is coached by Red Berenson. He's a Regina native and a Michigan grad who, when he was with the St. Louis Blues, once scored six goals in a single game. He played fifteen years in the NHL and coached the Blues for three more before returning twenty years ago to Ann Arbor to coach his alma mater. He has more than 500 victories for Michigan. Right now, his Wolverines are in first place in the twelve-team CCHA. MSU is third, but only two points behind, and the weekend should go a long way towards deciding who plays whom in the playoffs.

Comley comes from Stratford, Ontario. He's fifty-seven, slim and thoughtful. He played hockey at Lake Superior State. That's where he met Mason, who was his coach. Later, he coached there himself for three years, followed by twenty-six years coaching Northern Michigan before he succeeded Mason at Michigan State. Going into this season, Comley had won more than 600 college games.

After the practice, after he's showered and put on a sweater and slacks and looks casually professorial, Comley returns to rinkside to do a "double-ender" interview for a Fox Sports TV program called *Overtime* that will be broadcast before tomorrow's game. Fox isn't covering that game, the university TV network is, but Fox will carry Saturday night's game from the Joe Louis Arena in Detroit, an indication of just how important college hockey is in these parts. The anchor with whom Comley will be talking is in Seattle. At this end, there's just a cameraman and two producers. "Seattle's a hub, a Fox distribution point," one of the producers says. Comley, in a voice check after he's been wired up, asks whether it's raining out there. Seattle apparently tells him it isn't—you can't hear that end of the conversation without an earpiece—because Comley answers that that's good because when it's not raining it's hard to beat that part of the country.

They get going, and Comley says the standard stuff about a tough opponent and how important it is that MSU play its own game. But he does it matter-of-factly, easily and politely, and doesn't try to make it sound as if no one has ever said it before.

Sitting in his office after the Fox interview, Comley talks about his practices. "Each day, we prepare for our next opponent. We watch videos of their power play and practice our defense. We watch videos of their penalty killing and practice our power play. Then there's team play. So each day you're working on something."

Scouting, obviously, is a major factor in the Spartans' success. "The assistant coaches here do most of the early scouting," Comley says. "What I want them to do is filter it, come back to me with someone I *have* to see. But I do a lot on my own, too. Size is the last factor. If I want size, it's more on defense. I can live with twelve forwards who are five-nine to six feet, but in today's game you've got to have four or five defensemen who are six-one or six-two."

What bothers Comley, and presumably other coaches, is that recruiting a kid, like everything else, isn't as straightforward as it used to be.

"Nearly all the kids have agents now, even if some of them call themselves 'family advisers,' and I think they play a negative role," Comley says. "They and the families micromanage these kids like you wouldn't believe. They all think that they're going to be pros—at fourteen they think that they're going to be pros. It used to be that you got to know the youngster and his family, spent some time in the home, built up a relationship with them and they'd make a decision on you and the school. Now, it's a race to get in favor with all these 'advising groups' so that they'll recommend you. I've rejected kids because I wouldn't take the whole package; [they're] kids I don't want anything to do with because of the over-involvement of advisors and parents."

Next he turns to the difference between Canadian and American college hockey. "I'm not knocking the Canadian schools, but the hockey is better here," he says. "We're recruiting the best seventeen-year-old, eighteen-year-old and nineteen-year-old talent we can get. Canadian colleges are getting kids who played major junior, who wanted to be pros. It didn't work out, so they're back playing hockey as a secondary venture. Our kids still believe they're going to be pros, and they want an education to go along with it."

Comley is like every other good coach in that he wants kids with a "feel" for the game. "Once you see that they have that, that they know where to go on the ice, go to the good places instinctively, then you look at the other categories—Can they shoot? Are they good with the puck? What kind of skaters are they?"

He pauses. "Look, on offense, a winger might just barrel down the wing and go straight for the net. A kid with a feel for the game is going to go down the wing hard, take a read if he can beat the defenseman, and spin out if he can't—and make a pass if a pass is the right play. Some see the ice, some don't. Defensively, it's the same: you're not going to be a good defensive player if you're greedy and one-dimensional. You can teach and teach and teach, but unless a kid has grasp for the game, he'll never get it. A good defensive player is responsible.

"And it shows off the ice, too. Kids who know the game usually have their heads on straight, they don't cut corners, they know their responsibilities. There are an awful lot of kids that may be good enough to play here, but they can't handle the academics, they can't manage their time. My kids have to do that."

One of the best of them is Jim Slater, from Lapeer, which is between Lansing and Port Huron. He's the team's captain and leading scorer, a well-built, dark-haired twenty-one-year-old with that cheerful confidence young people have when they like what they're doing and they do it well. He was Atlanta's second pick, thirtieth overall, in the 2002 draft.

"I went to a prospect camp in Atlanta," he says. "College kids have to pay their own way. I was down there last summer and the summer before, skating and getting to know their organization. They were really good to me."

Before MSU, Jim played for the Cleveland Barons in the North American Hockey League, a Tier II junior league. "I committed to come here after my junior year in high school," he says. "One of the reasons was because of Coach Mason, and now that Coach Comley is here I'm learning something else from him. They're both great coaches. Coach Mason was more on the defensive side. Coming out of high-scoring junior, he taught me a lot about defense and how to play in my own end. Coach Comley gives me more of the offensive side, so I've got the best of both—offense and defense."

Slater says that a player's character is important. "On and off the ice, around the community, kids look up to you. How you present yourself, carry yourself, kids notice that, so you have to try to be a good person off the ice."

He's studying what he calls "human resources" (Human Resource Management), which, he says, "will help me with me with almost anything I want to do afterwards. We get tutors when we need them, but most of the games are close by here, so the most we ever miss is two days in a row, and that doesn't happen very often."

Jim's father, Bill, was a pro football player—a defensive line-man with the Minnesota Vikings and New England Patriots in the seventies. "My parents don't like to miss a game. They even came to Alaska with us," Slater says. "We left here at 6 a.m. and got there at 7 p.m." That was a two-day trip; they won one game, lost the other.

As far as his future goes (he has one more year at MSU), Jim says, "every kid thinks he has a good chance at the NHL, and I do." Is he prepared to play in the minors? "I'd give it a shot, because I don't want to give up that easily. I love hockey. I don't know where I'd be without it."

Michigan State enshrines its hockey history as it passes. On the walls around the rink upstairs are plaques, framed newspaper headlines celebrating victories, photographs of Spartan teams. There are also photos of the 1980 Olympic gold medal winners that Ron Mason and so many others credit with helping popularize hockey in the United States (even as the shortsighted NHL's bosses seem unable to capitalize on that popularity). There are also pictures of those who went on to the NHL, as well as such non-Spartans as Gordie Howe, shown shaking hands with a member of the 2001 MSU team. "We love Howe here," says a young man in the stands. He's watching his girlfriend. She's on the women's team that began practice after the men were finished. "Remember, this is Red Wings country," he points out. "Even guys like me, too young to have ever seen him, know all about him."

Ron Mason's stuff is up here, too, preserved in a glass case like a saint's relics: skates, gloves, warmup jacket, his whistle and one of the notebooks he'd use during practice.

"In our situation, memorabilia serves two purposes," says Tom Newton, the former Oshawa General, who is forty-seven and in his fourteenth year here as assistant coach. "Number one, it's part of our recruiting process. When we bring in young prospects and they see all those NHLers who went here—and that's more than sixty of them—it's gotta be impressive. The other part of it is the sense of pride the university has in its hockey program."

Three of Newton's teammates in Oshawa—Rick Middleton, Lee Fogolin and Greg Malone—played in nearly 3,000 NHL games between them. But after a full season in Oshawa, and parts of three others, Newton hung up his own NHL hopes and headed off to play at Bowling Green, where Mason was coaching. (In those days—the early 1970s—players could move from Junior A to U.S. universities because Junior A wasn't considered professional hockey.)

"The writing was on the wall in Oshawa," Newton says. "I was five-foot-nine, size was becoming important, and I wasn't having a lot of success there. But I still wanted to play, and I knew I was a good enough student that I could hold that end up. I knew how important [an education] was for my life."

Newton graduated with a BA in education, then got his master's, but didn't teach. He went right to hockey. He was an assistant at Bowling Green, then coached at Kent State and Western Michigan before rejoining Mason at MSU.

He believes that the caliber of play at the best U.S. hockey colleges is higher than Canadian major junior. "Our players are older than most of the juniors, and at that age it likely makes them stronger," he says. "They're just as skilled and probably a little more experienced. I know when the U.S. development team—the country's best teenagers out of Ann Arbor—played a lot of teams in the OHL [Ontario Hockey League] their record was pretty favorable."

Much of Newton's time is spent trying to recruit. "You go to games, check out the talent, speak to the coaches, research to see if the academics are in place," he says. "Obviously, you must check to see if they're eligible to play for MSU based on where they played before you saw them."

As he points out, ex-professionals from any level as well as former major junior players are ineligible. "It doesn't matter if it was only one exhibition game, he can't qualify."

Once a kid hits the campus in East Lansing, Newton says, there is a great support structure. "There are students and study halls—and remember, these are pretty good students coming in and they've made a commitment. Our team average right now is a B, so they work at it. They're given all the help they need, and if a kid is cut from the team strictly on his hockey performance, he has the option of staying at MSU and studying on his scholarship. If he gets in trouble and there are other issues, then his scholarship will be looked at, but MSU won't allow a scholarship to be taken away simply on athletic performance."

Newton has coached some awfully good players, many of whom went on to the NHL. But if he's forced to pick a favorite, it's Rem Murray. "He had over 50 points a year the four years he was here," Newton says. "He had such a well-rounded game. He could play center, he could play the wing. He played the power play and he killed penalties. He was such a reliable player. He left here with a degree in engineering, so he was a good student. I think he represents what college athletics should be all about: he got the total experience."

Another indication of the place that hockey has in the hearts of MSU and its friends is the existence of the MSU Blueline Club, a booster club that holds a lunch before each home game at Tripper's Sports Bar, in a shopping mall about ten minutes from the campus.

On the drive over, Ron Mason says, "I try to stay out of things now because it's Rick's show, but I've been asked to speak today." Then, musing about the game itself, he says, "I think they should get rid of the instigator rule. In the old days you stood up for yourself. Nobody likes brawling, but the odd bit of fisticuffs never really hurt anybody but at least players had a sense of what might happen to them—if I'm going to slam this person into the boards I'm going to pay a price for it. It makes sense."

Inside Tripper's, beyond the TV sets and pool tables and burly young patrons, is a big room called the Comedy Zone. About 200 Blueliners are here. Most them appear to be retirees in their sixties and seventies, so there is a lot of white atop MSU's forest green shirts and sweaters. They are sitting at long tables eating fried chicken, pasta salad and chocolate cake. On the walls are large, realistic sketches of David Letterman, Jerry Seinfeld, Bill Cosby and Steve Martin. They've never performed here, which is perhaps why the artist has given them somewhat bewildered smiles. The club's chairman gets up to pitch bus trips for the remaining out-of-town games, draws raffle winners for tickets, and then closes with, "Let's get the rink rockin' and rollin' tonight!"

Mason and Rick Comley are at the head table. Both get loud applause. Comley speaks first, quietly detailing what lies ahead, not only for tonight against Michigan but for the playoffs. When it's Mason's turn he talks about the recruitment of student athletes. He brings up the University of Colorado, which has been taking a beating in newspapers and on TV for treating high school footballers to drunken parties, strippers and sex; a couple of other schools have also been in the news because they've passed out money and cars. Mason says all this misconduct risks giving decent programs, such as MSU's, a bad name.

He turns to academics and says that MSU has 750 student athletes, men and women, in twenty-five sports. Their grade-point average is slightly higher than MSU's as a whole, and their graduation rate last year was 74 percent, compared with 68 percent for the rest of the university. "Out of 750, you're going to get ten or twelve who are dumb as hell," he says. "Unfortunately, they're the ones you hear about."

On the drive back to campus after lunch, after he's shaken about fifty hands, Mason brings up one of his concerns about what hockey players do to try to improve themselves. He says many of them feel that they can add muscle, and consequently strength, without upsetting their body. "Some players, instead of staying at their natural weight—say, 175 pounds, they're bulking up," he says. "I'm not talking necessarily about steroids—that's crazy and dangerous—but simply lifting weights. They build up all this muscle and their natural bone structure can't support it. I'm sure this leads to injuries. So I'd take this guy at five-foot-nine with great natural strength as long as he has the skill."

Then he gets back to how the NHL could improve its game. He says, "They took out the regrouping rule. That's why there are so many offsides. It used to be that once you cleared the zone you could go back in and attack. There was coaching involved. In the college game we have the regrouping rule and it's great. You'll see tonight."

MSU publicity says that the university has produced more Rhodes scholars in the last generation than any other Big Ten school. It's likely produced as many NHLers as any other Big Ten school, too—if not more. Among Spartans who have gone on to substantial careers, had more than the proverbial cup of coffee up there, are Craig Simpson, who played for Pittsburgh and Edmonton; the Miller brothers, Kevin, Kelly and Kip, who, among them, played with the Rangers, Washington, St. Louis and Detroit; Bryan Smolinski, five teams, including Los Angeles and Ottawa; Rod Brind'amour, Philadelphia and Carolina; Anson Carter, five teams including Washington and Edmonton; Mike York, Edmonton and the Rangers. And then there's Newton's favorite, Rem Murray, of Edmonton and Nashville. All were coached by Mason.

"Some of those guys stepped right into the NHL, never played a game in the minors," Mason says, singling out Joe Murphy, who played for Detroit and Chicago, and Kelly Miller. "One thing that helps is that it's a very competitive environment. We play only 34, 35 games, but they're all like playoff games. The whole year is a playoff. It's not like playing 60 or 70 games, where you can take a night off and it doesn't matter. You take a night off here and it could cost you your season. I tried to teach the kids the importance of hard work and the need to cooperate, because you're not on your own, you have teammates. Another thing is the socialization. The kid is here, in a university environment, for four years. He can't be traded, so it's up to us to make him the best he can be. I think I've done a lot for the guys I coached."

Michigan's Berenson has sent a passel of Wolverines to the NHL, too. Jeff Norton played nearly 800 games with eight teams. Marty Turco is Dallas's goalie. Mike Comrie returned to his hometown to play for the Oilers (he's since moved to the Phoenix Coyotes). John Madden is a New Jersey regular, and Chris Tamer, the Michigan native, is one of the toughest defensemen in the NHL and has been with Pittsburgh, the Rangers and Atlanta. Mike Knuble, after so-so seasons in Detroit and with the Rangers, has blossomed in Boston . . . and the list goes on.

Tonight the Munn Arena, as usual, is sold out. Paid admission is 6,812 and the crowd is as worked up and noisy as the basketball crowd was three nights before. Given the respective sizes of the two crowds, there seem to be fewer kids tonight, but perhaps more women; overall, it may be a slightly younger crowd. The MSU band is there, not as big as it was for basketball—the tuba section is down from eight to one. But in the smaller arena, the noise level is about the same.

The press box holds about thirty, and it's full—media from both universities and from Lansing and Ann Arbor and Detroit, print and broadcasting. Al Randall, from Trenton, Michigan, broadcasts for the University of Michigan. He's around fifty, stocky good-humored if a little hyper; he's just seen his daughter, a second lieutenant in the army, off to Iraq. "We had a party for her last night," he says. "I'm very proud of her."

Randall says he played junior hockey, then covered high school hockey in northern Michigan for twenty years. "My kids grew up with their dad always on the road," he says. Nine years ago, when his predecessor took a job with the Red Wings, Randall replaced him. "I love hockey," he says. "It's the best game in the world—and you want to know something? My first year broadcasting for Michigan, Red [Berenson] won his first national championship."

Ray Newton, the seventy-four-year-old father of the assistant coach, Tom Newton, and a retired school principal, is here from Uxbridge, Ontario, for the Michigan games. He says he tries to get down once a month or so. He was born and grew up in Port Arthur, Ontario, which, with Fort William, make up what is now the city of Thunder Bay. He played hockey with or against some formidable future NHLers, including Danny Lewicki and Dave Creighton. "But I wasn't that good," he says. "I hurt my knee playing football at fifteen, and it was never the same." As far as U.S. college hockey goes, he likes the wide-open game. "It's much more exciting than the NHL today," he says.

"To me, it's a much faster game, far superior to anything we have going. Just the fact that they don't allow brawling. You get into a fight and you're gone for at least one game, and maybe more."

Then Ray Newton makes the criticism heard more and more often about Canadian minor hockey: that there are too many games, that youngsters need to practice more to improve their skills. "I like the idea that [here] they're on the ice every day learning, practicing at least three, probably four days a week, then they have their games on weekends," he says. "I think that's far superior to having kids sixteen, seventeen years old playing—you know the major juniors, they can end up playing 100 games a year with exhibitions and playoffs. They're going to learn a lot more in practice. When Tom played for Oshawa, he'd be away—Sudbury, Ottawa, the Soo—for three or four days at a time."

A couple of dozen NHL scouts, half of whom seem to be wearing three-quarter-length black leather car coats, are lined up behind the top of row of seats, their cell phones and notebooks at the ready. Seventeen of the players below them have been drafted—ten Wolverines and seven Spartans—so they're checking on their progress and looking for fresh blood. The scouts are chatting and laughing with each other, not appearing to mind that this might be the 200th game they've seen this season. Nor do they give away much as far as who they're interested in. "It's better at this stage we keep things to ourselves," one of them says.

Among them is Jim Hammett, the chief scout for the Colorado Avalanche. He has nine scouts working under him, but he figures that he sees about 50 college games a year himself, plus the juniors and minor pros. Home for Hammett is Kelowna, B.C. "But there are so many teams and leagues now that it doesn't matter where you live, because you're always traveling," he says. One of the first things Hammett looks at is the skating. "This is the fastest game in the world," he says. "We have a saying: 'Slow is no go.' If a player can't skate, he can't play, in any pro league."

Hammett calls the MSU–Michigan rivalry one of his favorites. "It shows the way each team is up for the games," he says. It is games like this where scouts get a good look at a player's strengths, and his weaknesses. Hammett agrees with Tommy Newton that this hockey is generally somewhat better than major junior, which has its age limit of twenty. "Most of these college guys are older, in their twenties, and are a little more experienced and stronger," he says.

Along from Hammett is Paul Fenton, who played more than 400 NHL games and now is Nashville's director of player personnel. The most-talked-about Nashville signing for this season was Jordin Tootoo, the Inuk youngster from Rankin Inlet, just below the Arctic Circle. "Jordin never stops," Fenton says. "Scoring may not be his forte, but he's tough and he draws a lot of penalties. He's a ball of energy." Fenton likes college hockey, but says that Nashville also has some major-junior prospects. As a rule, unlike Hammett, he works close to his home in Springfield, Massachusetts. "There's so much going on in New England, I usually don't have to travel very far," he says.

Ron Mason is right about the game being more wide open because, except for icing, there is no red line; it makes many NHL games, with their stacked neutral zones that stifle play, seem unimaginative and dull by comparison. But it's also a bit scrambly, as both teams seem to be fighting first-period jitters and the period ends in a scoreless draw.

The second period is better, more disciplined. The University of Michigan's Jeff Tambellini opens the scoring about five minutes in. He lifts a hard backhand from in close, high over the shoulder of the MSU goalie on his stick side. Tambellini, a first-round draft pick of the Los Angeles Kings, is from B.C. and is the son of Steve Tambellini, the former NHLer who now works in the Vancouver Canucks' front office. Jeff was a member of Canada's junior team, but a man in the press box says he hasn't been scoring well since he got back from the world championships, in which Canada lost to the United States.

Keith Mollin, a 1966 University of Michigan graduate, is a retired university administrator. He figures 500 or 600 Michigan fans made the trip to East Lansing from Ann Arbor or Detroit. He says there would be more, but that it is hard to get tickets here and at Bowling Green, Northern Michigan, and Miami (Ohio) because hockey is so popular and the demand so high. "They go pretty quickly," he says. "Me, I like college hockey much better than the NHL; and you must remember, these kids all go to school. I've flown up with [University of Michigan players] to Alaska to mentor a kid on the flight for his final exams."

The second period has lots of scoring chances, which Ron Mason likes, and MSU ties the score. But then, in the period's last three minutes, Michigan scores twice and MSU once and the Spartans are down 3–2 at the intermission. Things turn for the better for MSU in the third period: by the midway mark, the Spartans have tied the game at 3–3, and a couple of minutes later they go ahead 4–3 on a goal by Mike Lalonde, who comes from a reserve in northern British Columbia. It's his 20th of the season.

Then, in what appears to be the icing on the cake for Michigan State, a Michigan player takes a holding penalty with a little more than two minutes left in the game. "Red must be going crazy," says a reporter in the press box. "What a stupid goddamn penalty to take at a time like this." The pro-MSU crowd is on its feet. Not only are the Spartans now bound to win, but their CCHA title hopes are still alive.

Yeah, right, as the kids say. The Wolverines, although a man short, have little choice but to pull their goalie. They do, and they storm the MSU net. With just over a minute left, and their man still in the penalty box, they score. The crowd's cheers are replaced by a hollow silence. The third period ends 4–4. Over-time solves nothing and, like the basketball crowd three nights ago, the hockey crowd is left sad and disbelieving.

The players line up at center ice to shake hands, a nice touch that college hockey has kept over the years regardless of the intensity of the game. But even from the stands, the Spartans' dejection is plain to see. Two camera crews and half a dozen reporters wait for Rick Comley in the press lounge after the game. He is gracious, although he makes it clear that this tie feels like a loss. "Of course I'm down," he says. "But watching those kids come off the ice dead tired was good. It showed it was an all-out effort. That's all you can ask from your team. It was college hockey the way you want it." And that was it for tonight.

Three or four MSU players arrive. They've showered and are dressed in jackets and ties. They speak politely and softly, like well-brought-up kids in front of adults but, as the crowd was doing thirty minutes before, they're shaking their heads in disbelief. One of them, A. J. Thelen, a defenseman from Savage, Minnesota, won't be eighteen until next week. He's a product of the development team. "I was breathing hard before the game even started," he says. "The adrenaline was really pumping."

The next afternoon, the team bus leaves the Munn Arena at two-thirty for the game against Michigan at the Joe Louis Arena, the home of the Red Wings. The ninety-minute drive takes the team through what used to be the heart of GM and Ford country, but there are lots of Toyotas and Nissans and Volks-wagens on the road. The players have been told to forget last night's game, that it's over; but they still feel spooked by it. "It's pretty devastating," Mike Lalonde says. "Sometimes it just doesn't go our way." Another player says, "What can you say? We blew it. We had it won and we blew it." In spite of this, however, the team says it feels up for tonight.

The bus parks in the alley that runs behind the Joe Louis. The alley is lined by lamp standards hung with Red Wings pennants. Inside the rear doors of the arena, on the wall, there is a souvenir—a big, old weather-beaten road sign directing drivers to the Olympia Stadium, the home of Red Wings triumphs before "the Joe" was built. And the hallways by the dressing rooms carry the names of Red Wings greats from Howe and Terry Sawchuk to Chris Chelios and Sergei Fedorov. One of the MSU players, Chris Snavely, is a defenseman from Lancaster, Pennsylvania, who began playing junior when he was only fourteen. He was a member of the U.S. Under-18 Select Team that won a silver medal at the 1999 Four Nations Cup in Prague, and he hopes to play professionally. He looks around the arena approvingly. "Yeah, this the kind of place I'd like to play in," he says.

Stocky, dark-haired Mike Lalonde and a handful of other players are in their hockey underwear and are pacing around outside the dressing room, waiting for the team's pregame stretching exercises. Coach Comley is leaning against a far wall of the hallway watching them, but leaving them alone, giving them some space before the game. He looks over at Lalonde. "He's a remarkable kid," he says. "He probably didn't have it easy."

So just how does a half-Cree, half-white youngster from the Saulteau reserve near Moberly Lake, an hour west of Dawson Creek in northern British Columbia, get to East Lansing, Michigan, and MSU? Lalonde shrugs and says, "Yeah, I guess

I didn't come from the typical background to get here. Maybe growing up on a reserve was kind of tough, but it was okay. My dad always had a job. We didn't have it hard." He says his father, although he didn't play much himself, was one of the driving forces in hockey for him. "Just rec hockey on the lake," he says. "But he was always pushing me to do the best I could in hockey and everything I did."

Lalonde has just turned twenty-four. He's in his junior year, which means he has one more. "It took me a while to get here." One of the reasons for this was a thigh injury that laid him up for nine months, including half of his last year of junior hockey with the Prince George Spruce Kings of the British Columbia Junior Hockey League, an injury that nearly cost him his leg. But it was while he was with the Spruce Kings that two of his former teammates—Brad Fast, from Fort St. John, B.C., later a Carolina draft pick, and Mike Stutzel, from Victoria, who signed with Phoenix—headed off to MSU and Northern Michigan, respectively. That's how Lalonde first learned of U.S. college hockey.

Len McNamara, the Spruce Kings GM, also had connections with the Spartans. The closer he got to being recruited, he says, the more excited he got. "And when I visited Michigan State, there was no doubt this was the place for me." What particularly impressed him "was to go into the Munn and see all those banners and championship pictures." His first MSU game isn't something he's likely to forget, either. It was the so-called Cold War, that outdoor game at Spartan Stadium before a crowd of nearly 75,000 against the University of Michigan.

His future, like that of most young hockey players, is still uncertain. "I don't know if the NHL is in my sights," he says, "but perhaps the AHL or other minor pros. Or I'd be happy to end my career here. I'll have to see."

At any rate, after he's out of hockey, he expects to go back to northern British Columbia and work in parks and recreation. "Maybe on a reserve," he says. "I think I'd like that." Earlier, Lalonde told a university sports reporter that "being Native American has always played a role in my life. It's a lot about family and doing things in groups. People stick together. Thinking about others has really helped to keep me levelheaded."

In the press lounge, where supper consists of pizza from Little Caesar's, which is owned by Mike Ilitch—who also owns the Red Wings—a man in late middle age is having a coffee. He's one of tonight's goal judges and he is also a goal judge for Red Wings games. He doesn't want to be quoted by name, because it's none of his business, but he says the stickwork in college hockey is much more severe than in the NHL. "They're right when they say that fighting cuts down on the stickwork," he says. "I'm not kidding when I say that I've never seen any- thing like it—spearing, slashing, butt-ends. I'm right against the glass; I see it all. They know they can get away with it because if someone takes a poke at them he's gone for the game."

A man with him says, "You'll never convince me. I think fighting is horseshit. The players are getting too big. It'll only take one punch and a guy falls on his head, helmet or not, and is seriously hurt. And what other sport allows fighting, anyway? All they gotta do is start calling the stickwork, all of it."

The game starts before a capacity crowd of 20,006. It's like the crowd last night at the Munn, noisy and good-humored, although it's more than three times bigger. MSU fans are dressed in their green, while dozens of Michigan fans wear bright, yellow curly wigs. The two college's bands are here, at opposite ends of the rink, and MSU's is up to three tubas. "This is huge game," says a young woman rushing around the press box and passing out lineups. "It's always sold out—always." About fifty people are there, including the Fox TV broadcast crew and some Red Wings personnel. The scouts, in their black leather car coats, are back. The Maple Leaf, as it does at the Munn Arena, hangs alongside the Stars and Stripes.

Midway into the third period, MSU has withstood five Michigan power plays and there is still no score. Up in the press box a fair, portly man in early middle age catches his breath over every close play. He says he shouldn't be taking sides, being with a broadcast crew, "but I gotta say I'm leaning towards State." He gasps a couple of more times, then says, "Something was wrong with my blood, but they couldn't find out here what it was. Finally I was sent to the hospital at MSU and they discovered I had leukemia. They treated me, and I've been clear for seven years—seven years—so I can't help hoping for them."

Just then, as if in answer to a prayer, Mike Lalonde scores from a scramble close in. The man who had leukemia, remembering that he's in the press box, is quietly ecstatic—there's no cheering or dancing. MSU holds on to win, 1–0.

"It was bouncing around in the slot and I just took a whack at it," Lalonde says later. "A goal like that, in this atmosphere, is huge."

Afterwards, the two coaches each say nice things about the other team. Red Berenson also says there isn't much satisfaction in his team winning the CCHA title. The Wolverines did it tonight because, in spite of their loss, second-place Miami

(Ohio) also lost. "You can't feel good about backing into it," Berenson says.

Outside, the MSU players, after passing through about fifty fans waiting there to congratulate them, board the bus, each with a Little Caesar's pizza in his hand.

The bad night still isn't over for Berenson. As the Spartans' bus moves slowly through the traffic towards Interstate 96 and Lansing, the Michigan bus can be seen up ahead, stopped by a corner. It apparently clipped a car that was parked where it shouldn't have been. The car is empty and no one is around. Although it's raining hard, a man with no raincoat gets out of the Michigan bus to check the car and see what happened. Under the streetlights the man, with his fifties crewcut, the same one that he wore for years as an NHL player, can be seen clearly. The MSU bus swings gingerly by, and a member of the MSU staff, looking out, says, "Poor Red." He really means it.

In late March 2004, Minnesota-Duluth knocked MSU out of the regional playoffs. Michigan beat New Hampshire, but then lost in overtime to Boston College.

CHAPTER 7

Back to School

PETERBOROUGH, ONTARIO • Outside, the afternoon is hot and sunny; inside, the air-conditioning is going full-blast. About thirty eleven- and twelve-year-olds in full hockey equipment, except for skates and helmets, are sitting in the large room above the two rinks in the Evinrude Centre, one of the city's four hockey arenas. They're at hockey school. Soon they'll be on the ice, but right now they're listening to a tall, well-built young man wearing a baseball cap over his long, black hair, shorts and a T-shirt—dressed more for the tennis court than the rink.

"Too often, a defenseman going back is looking for the big hit," the young man is saying, "and just as often the guy skates around him. You've got to remember that playing the body is more than the so-called big hit. It's using your body to block a player—slow him up, to steer him into the corner."

The speaker is twenty-six-year-old Mike Martone. Relaxing with a soft drink after he's finished his talk, he says the play of the Europeans who are here now, with their concentration on skills, is good for hockey. "I watch these kids and I wish I'd been that good when I was their age," he says. "We realize now that we can't play our old style because of the Europeans."

Martone is, and was, pretty good, though. He played four years of major junior with the Peterborough Petes and was their captain in his final year. A stay-at-home defenseman who took his share of penalties, he was a fourth-round pick of the Buffalo Sabres in 1996. When Buffalo didn't exercise its option, he signed a three-year contract with the Phoenix Coyotes and played those three seasons with the Mississippi Sea Wolves of the East Coast Hockey League. (The competition in that league included many fighting aquatic creatures: the Tallahassee Tiger Sharks, Louisiana Ice Gators, Baton Rouge Kingfish and South Carolina Stingrays.) Martone also had a handful of games with Springfield of the American Hockey League, but even those weren't enough to convince him that he had a decent shot at getting much further—researchers have put the odds of a player going from minor hockey to any kind of a National Hockey League career at 4,000 to 1—so when the Phoenix contract was up, Martone went back to school.

"It was tough to give up the NHL dream, but I had to be realistic," he says. "It wasn't that I didn't like it. Heck, I loved it, playing down there in Biloxi. The fans were wonderful. We'd get four, five thousand to a game. The team had been there three years by the time I got there, and the fans knew the game and they loved their Sea Wolves. They had an NHL exhibition game there, but the fan support wasn't as strong as it was for us, because the NHL is so far away. Even if the caliber of play was much better, they'd rather watch us.

"It was just that I didn't want to find myself at thirty-three or something, still slugging away down there with no chance of moving up. I've already had surgery on both hips, and I knew that I needed something to fall back on after hockey. The way I see it, I'm still young enough to play some more, after I get my education. If I'm ever asked for advice, I say that if you're coming out of junior and you don't have an NHL contract, get your education. You can always come back and play somewhere. There are so many leagues now, in the States, in Europe. My dad was born in Italy, so I'm trying to get over there. I might as well play as long as I can."

The school Martone chose, or that chose him, is St. Francis Xavier University. It's in the town of Antigonish, on the northeastern shore of Nova Scotia, halfway between Halifax and Sydney. The local Roman Catholic diocese started St. FX 150 years ago for the families of the county's fishermen and farmers and of the miners on nearby Cape Breton Island. It's nondenominational now, and has about 4,000 full-time students— almost the same as the number of people in Antigonish itself—and is undergoing an $85-million rebuilding plan that includes a business school and a $23-million science and engineering center.

But in spite of the glamorous new projects, there's still a lot of red brick, some ivy, and, when it's not snowing, lots of green grass. It looks like the kind of place where you could learn without getting lost and, for the second year in a row, *Maclean's* magazine gave St. FX top spot in its annual rankings of universities that cater primarily to undergraduates.

In the spring of 2004, he graduated with a Bachelor of Science degree in kinesiology and biology, which he completed in three years rather than four. "I've chipped away at it over the years," he says, by studying at Peterborough's Trent University when he was with the Petes and taking correspondence courses in the summers through Alberta's Athabasca College.

"I can look back and say that maybe I should have given the NHL shot a couple of more years," Martone says. "But I'd already given it six or seven, counting junior, so right now I'm happy with what I decided to do."

Under Canadian university rules, anyone who has received any money at all for playing, whether as a minor professional or major junior (major junior players get a couple of hundred dollars a week, an amount that varies according to experience) are ineligible to play during their first year at school. So Martone, and others like him, keep sharp by playing for local senior teams.

Martone comes from Sault Ste. Marie, a long way from Peterborough. He says that when he was growing up, his family always made schooling a priority. "I left home at sixteen to play hockey," he says. "Leaving your mom and dad at that age, you learn to grow up, learn a lot of things. It's not textbook learning, but it's just as important. I was fortunate to come to the Petes. They're a great organization. They got me a great billet and, like back at home, they emphasized school. You skip school, you don't play that night."

When he was a kid in the Soo, he says, he had his favorites in hockey—"What kid doesn't?"—but the person he looked up to most, and still does, has nothing to with hockey. "My father is my hero," Martone says. "When I was growing up, he worked at three jobs for the family. The way I look at it is that if I'm lucky enough to be able to play hockey, I owe it to myself to work as hard as he did. When I went to practice, I always gave it everything I had. It's the same in games. You might not be the most skilled player, but you can always work hard. Like I said, you owe yourself that."

Flash forward seven months, and Mike Martone is where he'd hoped and prayed that he'd be in late March—in Fredericton, New Brunswick, on the St. John River. The provincial capital, Fredericton traces its history back to the late seventeenth century, and there are cemeteries full of United Empire Loyalists to prove it. The city is home to about 50,000 people and a mixture of graceful colonial and rigid Victorian architecture, including the neo-Gothic Christ Church Cathedral, built in the mid-1800s. There are trees—Fredericton likes to call itself the City of Stately Elms—and parks, some high-tech industry, a couple of telephone call centers, and two universities, the University of New Brunswick and St. Thomas University.

Fredericton is hosting the 2004 Canadian Interuniversity Sports (CIS) hockey championship, and all of its approximately 1,500 hotel rooms have been booked for weeks. Besides St. FX, the contending teams are the University of Alberta Golden Bears (the favorites, with a season record of 39–0–2), the University of Ottawa Gee-Gees, Toronto's York University Lions, the Dalhousie University Tigers, from down the road in Halifax, and the UNB Varsity Reds.

This morning, Martone is working out with the St. FX X-Men at UNB's 4,000-seat Aitken University Centre, the site of the games. The rink is named for Lord Beaverbrook. Born Max Aitken in Ontario, but raised in New Brunswick, Beaverbrook—who makes Conrad Black, the latest Canadian peer, look like a second-stringer—was a British Member of

Parliament before he was named to the House of Lords. He owned three major British newspapers, was a member of British cabinets during both world wars and was a confidant of prime ministers David Lloyd George and Winston Churchill. He died in 1964, but the Beaverbrook Foundation has continued to give money to the University of New Brunswick as well as other provincial institutions, which is why the Beaverbrook name is attached to a few things in Fredericton: the Lord Beaverbrook Hotel, the Beaverbrook Art Gallery, the Lady Beaverbrook Rink, the Lady Beaverbrook Residence at UNB, and the Sir Max Aitken Pool. The foundation endowed a the-ater—the Playhouse—and there's a street near the university named Beaverbrook Court.

Being the resolute and resourceful competitor that he was in business, publishing and politics, Beaverbrook would likely approve of the young men fighting for this hockey champi-onship on his home ice.

But these teams are a far cry from those of a generation ago, when they might have been made up of teenagers and early-twenty-somethings who would have been playing for their high schools in High River or Gananoque or Upper Musquodoboit a year or two before. And they're here from every province— seven Albertans, for example, are on the UNB Varsity Reds; four Quebecers play for Dal—and from Minnesota, New York, Pennsylvania and the Czech Republic. The most recent CIS champions include l'Université du Québec à Trois-Rivières (in 2001 and 2003), the University of Western Ontario (in 2002), the University of Alberta (in 1999 and 2000) and UNB (in 1998).

Martone rates the level of play here as a step up from major junior, and only a small step down from the ECHL. Most of the players, he points out, played in the Ontario, Quebec or Western leagues, and many of them have played at least some pro hockey. And they're big—bigger than the junior players because they're older—and they're stronger. The York Lions have ten players who stand over six feet and weigh more than 200 pounds, led by Rich Kearns, formerly of the Brampton Battalion of the OHL, who comes in at six-six and 225. Dalhousie has twelve players at least six feet and 200, and even Alberta and Ottawa, with the fewest, have seven and eight, respectively. Mike Martone is six-three and 210, and he's not even St. FX's biggest player—that would be Wes Jarvis, from Ottawa, who was signed by the New York Rangers. A defenseman who played junior in Kitchener, he's a three-year veteran of Canada's national team, the AHL and the ECHL. Jarvis is six-four and 225.

"I loved the national team," he says. "We were based in Calgary, but we traveled around the world, playing in tournaments—in Russia, Japan, everywhere in Europe. It was great fun. I wouldn't have missed it for anything."

When he got back, he played with Charlotte and with Hartford, the Rangers' AHL farm team. "I was twenty, but most of the guys [with Hartford] were in their late twenties and thirties," he says. "The Rangers weren't developing any young players."

There's another Rangers experience that Jarvis won't forget. He and some other players were taking their physicals at Madison Square Garden on September 11, 2001, the day of the terrorist attacks on the World Trade Center. "The staff was just freaking out," he says. "They thought that the Garden might be a target. I left around 11:30, and all the buildings had been evacuated, and people were wandering around in shock. Some of them were waiting to use pay phones because their cell phones couldn't get through with the towers down. I can still see that glazed, empty look in their eyes.

"We were about half a mile away, and we saw the smoke, but when we got back to our hotel, from up high we could see the fires, see everything. We couldn't get out of Manhattan for three days. And I've never seen anything like the line of supplies going by the hotel—eighteen-wheeler after eighteen-wheeler going past, with medical supplies, construction equipment to clean up—a nonstop convoy."

Jarvis says that that night, he and some other players walked over to Times Square. "It was the weirdest feeling—not a light, not a car, not a person, except for cops on the corners," he says. "They told us to go home, get out of there."

The lounge at the Aitken Centre looks down on the rink. It is ringed with UNB hockey photos. Twenty-eight-year-old Jeff Andrews, after watching the Varsity Reds practice, is checking out the picture of the 1998 championship team he was on. He's pretty big, too, well over six feet. A left winger, Andrews is from Oshawa, and he played for the Generals and North Bay Centennials in the OHL before coming to New Brunswick. He has his bachelor's degree, and after playing a season for Tupelo, Mississippi, and Lake Charles, Louisiana, in the Western Professional Hockey League (which has since merged with the Central league). "I had a good year, scored a point a game and fought a lot," he says. He quit hockey to work three years in the Caribbean for Nortel. Now he's back at UNB, studying for his MBA, but his college hockey eligibility has run out.

Andrews runs his finger along the picture. From below come the muffled sounds of Martone and the rest of St. FX, who have the ice now. "We had a truly amazing team," he says, with excitement and pride in his voice. "That's Mike Kelly—he coached in North Bay and with the world juniors. Daryl Rivers played for the Ottawa 67s and London Knights; beside him is Jason Campbell, captain of Owen Sound. That guy's an RCMP officer . . . That's me—I was drafted by Toronto. Next is Brian Stewart, drafted by Los Angeles . . . that's Dax MacLean—he's UNB's all-time leading scorer. He quit hockey to look after his kids. Craig Menard plays for Shreveport. That's Ryan Lindsay—he was captain of the Oshawa Generals. Scott Cherrey was a second-rounder with Washington . . . We'd leave for class at 8 in the morning and not get back from the library until 10 at night. We'd practice from 3 to 7:30." He pauses. "We were a very close team. I hope at least some of these guys get back here this weekend. I haven't seen some of them since the team broke up."

Andrews likes the college game more than major junior. "Guys aren't trying to prove themselves by knocking someone's head off," he says. But he has reservations, too. "Because there's no fighting, there's lots of stickwork, just like everyone says. The fans don't see that, but the players do—wrists black and blue from slashes, their groins all bruised from spearing."

Still looking at the photograph, he says, "I guess I made the right decision to leave hockey when I did, but I miss it. Y'know, I really love hockey."

Later, in the same room, the head coaches and team captains are introduced to the media. The captain of the York Lions is Sean Murphy, from Aurora, just north of Toronto. For the reception, he's dressed in a jacket and tie and his blond hair is almost neat. He's very polite; he's also very serious. In a tournament like this, one loss can finish you. York's first game is tomorrow, against Dalhousie. When's he's told that Dal is worried about York's speed, particularly when the Lions break out of their own end, he nods. "That's good," he says. "Try to keep them off balance."

Murphy has sound hockey genes. His father is Mike Murphy, the former NHL player—with St. Louis, the Rangers and Los Angeles—and ex–Maple Leafs coach. One brother, Ryan, is with the Albany River Rats in the AHL, while another, Patrick, plays for Northern Michigan University.

A defenseman, Sean Murphy played for the Toronto St. Michael's Majors in the OHL, and went to a Tampa Bay Lightning camp in 2000. Texas's Laredo Bucks of the Central Hockey League have been after him, and he's also looking at possibilities elsewhere in the CHL and the ECHL. But like most of the other young men here, he says he wants a worthwhile alternative to hockey. In his case, he plans to be a teacher. "I don't mind playing in the minors—traveling around, living out of a suitcase—but I also want to be in a position to do something else," he says. "I don't want to have to depend on hockey for everything. I need something that I can use the rest of my life. But right now my goal is to try to make the AHL. I think that's a pretty realistic goal. Obviously, I'd love to play in the NHL, I'm not leaving that out, but I also want to set a real goal. If that doesn't work out, then I'll go down and play in the Central league or the East Coast league."

That night, the players and about 200 others are at a dinner in a huge room at the Fredericton Inn, the city's biggest hotel.

It's the annual Canadian Interuniversity Sport gala banquet. The former NHL star Frank Mahovlich, who is now a senator, is on hand, too. Apart from a couple of speeches, almost everything is in both English and French: "O Canada," the welcoming addresses, grace, what have you—which not only reflects New Brunswick's status as Canada's only officially bilingual province, but the presence of many Quebecers and other French-Canadians scattered among all the teams.

The guests of honor include a team of twelve-year-olds, the Brockton Boxers, from suburban Boston. They've been invited here to play a "Friendship Series," an attempt to make up for the terrifying reception they suffered last year in Montreal when, after they arrived for a tournament, their bus was surrounded by a screaming crowd protesting the United States' invasion of Iraq. Later, spectators booed "The Star-Spangled Banner" when it was played. "It was frightening," a parent said at the time. The reception couldn't have been more different on this trip. Two days ago, when the Boxers' bus crossed the border from Calais, Maine, into St. Stephen, New Brunswick, hundreds of young Canadian hockey players lined St. Stephen's main street, tapping their hockey sticks and chanting, "USA! USA!" Brockton's mayor, Jack Yunits, is traveling with the team. "Our young people here are just walking on air," he says.

The university hockey players are all dressed up—suits and ties, their hair gelled—looking neat and respectable, in spite of the wispy beards many of them have grown for the tournament. Wes Jarvis, Mike Martone and five teammates are at one table. Two of the five—Troy and Mike Smith—are brothers from Hamilton who both played in the OHL before coming to St. FX. The others are Blake Robson, from Calgary, a center who played five years in the WHL for Prince George and Portland; Dwayne Bateman, from Marmora, near Peterborough, is a goalie who was with St. Mike's and Plymouth; and Ryan Walsh, from Orleans, outside Ottawa, is a center, who also played for St. Mike's and followed Bateman down here.

In spite of the pressure of the tournament—and it's Troy Smith and Mike Martone's last year of eligibility—the players appear remarkably relaxed and comfortable.

Martone credits good team chemistry. "Everyone here came together like one big family," he says. "Sometimes that can be as important as having a good team. I'm lucky; it was like that with the Petes and in Mississippi, and we won there. As soon as I got here, we all seemed to hit it off, and as the year went on, we got closer and closer. And we were playing well, and that helps, too. I know there are teams where the guys don't get on, and it shows on the ice."

The next day, the first day of the tourney, St. FX plays Dalhousie. The rink is full—nearly 4,000 people. Down below, Dwayne Bateman, the goalie, is pacing in the corridor—in his underwear—outside the X-Men's dressing room. "We've beaten Dal nine times in a row," he says, "so you gotta wonder that it might end." Martone chimes in, "There's some bad blood between us. They do a lot of banging and crashing, even when they know they've lost."

Mike Mole, another OHL veteran (with Mississauga and Belleville) who has also played for Lowell in the AHL, is the starting goalie for St. FX today. Bateman is his backup. The X-Men go 3-for-9 on the power play and beat Dal, 5–0. Bateman is the first player off the bench to congratulate Mole on the shutout.

Someone tells Martone that he played a good game and notes that he made some fancy moves a couple of times when he took the puck deep into the Dalhousie zone. Martone, who had 1 goal and 7 assists in 27 regular season games—which are actually pretty good numbers for a defensive defenseman—laughs. "No kidding! Well you don't see that very much," he says.

St. FX has the next day off, but they have an early-morning skate. The afternoon game that day pits Dalhousie against York. Because the Tigers lost to St. FX, if they don't win today any hopes they have for a medal are gone. Around 11 o'clock, with the game still two hours away, Brad Pierce, a defenseman with Dalhousie, is in his sweats, stickhandling with a small ball, in a hallway in the nearly-empty Aitken Centre.

"This is part of a pregame routine," Pierce says, moving the ball around. He is twenty-three, six-two and 230 pounds. He played four years in the OHL—for St. Mike's, Barrie and, for two and a half years, North Bay. He comes from Brampton, and he's one of eight Dalhousie players from Ontario. "There are five guys at this tournament that were on my team in North Bay," he says. "When I decided to go back to school, I had a choice between the Ontario schools and the Atlantic schools, and I chose Dal because it's a better league down here. I also knew that Halifax was a great city, and I wanted to experience more of Canada." He's studying business. "I have two more years here, and then I think I'd like to try the pros somewhere."

Dal, seeded fifth, beats Sean Murphy's third-seeded York Lions, 4–2. They come back from trailing 2–0 with a pair of goals in forty-one seconds at the end of the second period. Graham Wise, the York coach, says that when Dal scored its third goal, "It was like being hit in the back of the head with a two-by-four. Even though we kept working hard, it just seemed to take everything out of us." In the evening game, UNB beats Ottawa, 5–2. Ottawa had already lost to Alberta, 7–3, on the opening day, so the Gee-Gees are finished.

Earlier that evening at around five-thirty, before a team meeting at their hotel, the X-Men head out for a meal. They go to a bar and restaurant called the Hilltop, which deserves better than its location in a strip mall just off the highway to Saint John. By five o'clock the Hilltop is jammed, there isn't a parking spot to be had, and at least fifty people are lined up into the street waiting to get in. At least the weather is good. "Best place in town on a Friday night," says a man at the end of the line. Inside are pine tables, deep booths and waitresses with heavy trays, long legs and tired smiles. St. FX has reservations, and the menu seems pretty well set: club sandwiches, pasta salad and tea or juice.

The coach of St. FX is stocky with red hair and a close-cropped red beard that make him look Irish, which is as it should be, seeing as his name is Danny Flynn. On his way to a booth with two of his assistant coaches, he shakes half a dozen hands. This is his ninth year coaching the X-Men, and he has never won a CIS championship. In both 2001 and 2003, his team lost in the final to Trois-Rivières.

Flynn comes from Dartmouth, and he played hockey for St. FX. He spent two years in Newfoundland playing senior hockey for the Grand Falls Cataracts and working for the province's hockey association. Then he returned to Nova Scotia for six years, playing senior hockey for the Dartmouth Moosehead Mounties and working for the Nova Scotia amateur hockey association. In the fall of 1987, he joined the OHL's London Knights as an assistant coach. "I remember loading up my Honda Prelude," Flynn says. "A friend of mine, Donn Matheson, a school principal who scouts for Boston, came with me. Donn comes from Glace Bay, and as we're driving across the top of Toronto [along Highway 401], he says, 'Jesus, Danny, the only thing with sixteen lanes in Glace Bay is the bowling alley.'"

From London, Flynn went to Sault Ste. Marie for five years as an assistant to Ted Nolan, and was on hand for the Greyhounds' Memorial Cup year in 1993.

"The Soo is an unbelievable hockey town," he says. "And the people really go that extra mile to make you feel at home. And if you love hockey, there's no better place in the whole world. We've lived in lots of places, but my wife will tell you that hands down the very best place we've lived is Sault Ste. Marie."

Flynn says that Nolan, who was let go as coach by Buffalo in 1997, should be back in the NHL. But because his differences with Sabres GM John Muckler led to Muckler's getting fired, "He's been frozen out by the veteran GMs. You see lots of other coaches get second chances. What Ted needs is a young GM who's not in that tight, tight circle."

The best player Flynn says he coached in the OHL was Adam Foote, the Colorado defenseman who played in the Soo. "The things about Foote were that he was an exceptionally good skater and two, what set him apart from others, was that he was so competitive. Whether it was cards in the back of the bus, or puck races in practice, or a game for two points, he played for keeps."

The best player he coached against in the OHL, he says, was the late Bryan Fogarty, who died after years of abusing drugs and booze. "He had all the tools to become an NHL Hall of Famer. There were lots of good players who came through the OHL when I was there, such as Eric Lindros and company, but for a player who absolutely dominated the league, controlled the game every second he was on the ice, I'd have to say Bryan Fogarty."

Flynn turns to St. FX, speaking quickly, enthusiastically, the words spilling out in a rush. "I scout two ways: I'm a scout for L.A., so I can tap their network and I can call coaches in major junior. I go up to Ontario at least twice a year. This year, I saw fifteen teams over Christmas. I scout the Quebec league pretty heavily, because it has teams in Sydney and Halifax."

This year's team has fifteen players from Ontario, six from Nova Scotia and one each from Newfoundland and Labrador, Quebec, Saskatchewan and Alberta. Flynn says he's going to go after more westerners. "There are so many great kids out there and so few schools, I think you'll see us try to recruit more western kids. Both UNB and Acadia have a lot of them."

Then Flynn tells a story about John Brophy, an Antigonish native he's known for years, when Brophy was coaching the Maple Leafs in the late eighties. "I was an assistant with London, and we were in Toronto for an afternoon game against the Marlies at Maple Leaf Gardens," Flynn says. "After the Leafs finished their morning skate, I went in to see Brophy. I said 'Broph, it's my first game as a major junior coach. Have you any advice?' and Brophy says, 'Kid, make goddamn sure you get good players.' All the years I've been coaching, I haven't received any better advice than that."

A recruiting rule Flynn now lives by is that he must see the player himself, something that keeps him on the road a lot. "Some guys will take kids on recommendation alone," he says. "I've had tough luck with kids I haven't seen myself. If you make a mistake, there's not much you can do about it. It's not as if you can trade him or put him on waivers. He's here for four years. It's hard, but I do my best to see every kid play so I know what's happening.

"But when you recruit, when you're after a kid, you can do your best with him and his parents, but the very best recruiters are other kids. You might go to a kid in Ottawa and ask him to come to St. FX. If he's resourceful, he's going to talk to kids he knows who are already there, or another kid will come to me and say, 'Pick him' or 'Don't pick this guy.'

"This is the fun part of the season. The hockey season is competitive, but the recruiting season is far more competitive and it last twelve months. I'm like Brophy; I need good players and I work hard to get them, but so do the other coaches. When it comes to coaches, there are no dogs in this league."

Martone got to know Flynn years ago in the Soo. "He was with Teddy, coaching the Greyhounds, and I was playing bantam and midget before I went to Peterborough. Later, one of my buddies, Kurt Walsh, who was at the Buffalo camp with me, came down here and I went to Mississippi. When I was finished there, I talked to Kurt and he told me how great it was here with Danny, that he really loved it, so I was lucky enough to get here."

Flynn continues: "I target guys twenty, twenty-one [years old]. Some have been to NHL camps, some may have played pro. I may go to them and say, 'If you're a good student and the

East Coast league looks like your best option for pro hockey, here's an alternative you might consider. It's a number one university, you'll play in a first-rate facility [St. FX's new rink, with a capacity near 1,800] that's often sold out, you'll get an education you can be proud of.' But it's hard. They have to pass their courses, probably take out a student loan. So the kids who come to this school are very committed, and when it's over I guarantee them that at a minimum they can go back to the East Coast league."

Unlike in the U.S., prospective players don't sign a letter of intent to play university hockey. "Most of the time it's a verbal commitment and a handshake between you and a boy," Flynn says. He says he's narrowing in on one particular prospect. "Having said that, there's always the chance that an offer may come along and he'll decide to go pro. So it's different than junior hockey, with the draft, or signing him up, like in the States. You keep your fingers crossed and stay in touch with him on a regular basis. If they sign a pro contract, you wish them well because they've chased down a lifelong dream. There's a lot of hard work and a little bit of luck, scouting at this level."

Flynn is talking so much that he's barely touched his food, but the waitress brings more iced tea or juice or whatever he's drinking. "And I've been lucky that I've coached with the national program six different times," he says, "so I have a fairly decent network in Europe, and I've been able to place a fair number of our kids there."

Another thing that Flynn stresses is the benefit of coaching in a small town, the kind, he says, that 99 percent of the players come from anyway. "The kids arrive in September, and their parents tell them that they'll see them at Christmas or April," he says. "In other words, they can't go running home to Mom and Dad on weekends. They grow up together."

As for coaching, Flynn says he doesn't think there is any one way to do it; everybody's style is different. "You coach inside your personality, apply your own style. I was with Teddy for five years, and I saw him yell at the kids once—once, in five years. Other guys say that in junior you gotta be yelling all the time, but that wasn't his way, and I think he was the same in the NHL. Then look at someone like Pat Burns. He's a fiery, in-your-face kind of guy, and he gets good results, so I don't think there's any one cookbook for doing it."

Flynn worries that university hockey doesn't get the respect and recognition it deserves in Ontario and parts of the west, where major junior and pro hockey are predominant. "When I coached in London with the Knights, Western had a heck of team," he says. "We'd get the full front page of sports and they'd be on page seven, six or seven lines. Down here, there are three major junior teams (Halifax, Sydney and Moncton), but we're not near any of them. We're the only game in town, and the crowds are great and the fans are beginning to realize just how good college hockey is."

As the players get up from their tables and booths and make their way to the door, most of Flynn's food lies cold on the plate. "Hockey has always been my game," he says. "I played lacrosse and baseball but hockey was the game I loved. There's nothing better than playing, but the closest thing you can get to it when you're finished playing is coaching. I like the inter-action with the kids and I like going to head-to-head with another coach to see who comes out on top."

Later that evening, after the team meeting, some of the St. FX players go to an alumni reception for them at another hotel, the Delta, on the banks of the St. John River. It's a balmy evening, more like May than March, and about a hundred St. FX graduates are there, ranging in age from their twenties to their sixties. Dave Smith, the father of Troy and Mike Smith, the brothers from Hamilton, is there, too. He's not an alumnus; he flew in to see his sons play. "I'm very proud of them," he says. "They're nice kids, and as far as hockey goes, they play hard, and you're not going to find them whining or anything like that. They're always focused on what they're doing. That's the way they've always been."

At fifty-six, Smith seems to be as focused on hockey as he says his sons are. He's a former radio broadcaster in southwestern Ontario who now handles publicity and marketing for Flamboro Downs, a raceway near Hamilton. He was also involved in hockey for more than thirty years as a coach, scout and executive, including a turn as GM and director of hockey operations for the minor-pro Brantford Smoke in what was then the Colonial Hockey League (and is now the United league).

Troy and Mike are nice-looking young men, and look like brothers, although Troy, at six feet and 200 pounds, is bigger than Mike. Troy is a defenseman. He played for four years in the OHL with the Detroit and Plymouth Whalers before coming to St. FX. He's graduating with his BA this spring, but wants to stay with hockey, perhaps becoming an on-ice official when he's finished playing.

Mike, who plays right wing, is one of the team's best skaters. He's studying sociology and criminology. Before St. FX he played with the Moncton Wildcats of the QMJHL, and with the Whalers and Kingston Frontenacs. He was Kingston's leading scorer two years ago. He began his serious hockey at Culver Military Academy in Culver, Indiana.

Dave Smith heard about Culver from a teacher there, whom he ran into at a hockey tournament. "Then a friend of mine, Pat Stapleton, the old Chicago Blackhawk, told me that it was a great hockey program and that he knew the coach, Al Clark," Smith says. Clark, who comes from Thunder Bay [Port Arthur], was a Toronto Maple Leafs draft pick, has his master's degree from the University of New Hampshire and used to be the head of Culver's mathematics department. He has been coaching for Culver ever since hockey began there in 1977, and his teams have produced seventeen NHL draftees, including Gary Suter, who played seventeen years in the NHL for Calgary, Chicago and San Jose, and John-Michael Liles of the Avalanche, a Culver teammate of Mike's. (And, Mike Smith points out, George Steinbrenner, the New York Yankees owner, went there, too.)

"Mike and I drove down," Dave Smith says. "At first we thought we'd gone to the wrong place because it comes out of nowhere. You're driving this country road, through these corn-fields—I've never seen corn as high, looked about eight or nine feet—and suddenly out of nowhere is this beautiful property. We thought it had to be Notre Dame, because we knew South Bend wasn't far away. But we went in and it was Culver, and after about half an hour Mike said he wanted to go." Mike was fourteen. "It was tough at first, at that age, being so far away from his family, but he did well." He played there four years—for the junior varsity team, then the Varsity B team, and the final two years with the Varsity A team. "He was the leading scorer on each team," Dave says.

"Antigonish is a small town, like Culver," Mike Smith says. "Coming here was like being back in high school. Everybody got on well. I figured if it could be like that, it'd be great, because those were some of my best times."

Dave says that Mike was not quite two when he skated for the first time. "I got the smallest skates I could, and even then I had to put cotton wool in the toes," he says. "We went to a local arena, and he was literally running on the ice. He'd go twenty-five or thirty feet and fall on his face, and he'd get up and start again. He never cried once. In fact, the only time he cried was when I wanted to take him off the ice and go home."

Young Mike loved watching Troy and another older brother play. "He'd go down to the arena and want to stay all day," Dave says. "Troy was, and continues to be, almost like a mentor, somebody Mike really looks up to. And Troy has taught Mike so much—not only about the game, but how to handle himself. They're very, very close. I've often thought that Troy doesn't get the recognition he deserves. He's come through a lot."

As a child Troy suffered a serious kidney problem that required an experimental operation to fix; when he was being scouted for junior hockey, he stepped on a puck and ended up having knee surgery; he's also broken his jaw and lost teeth. "He plays what I consider a quiet game," his father says. "He doesn't make a lot of mistakes, he's very smooth, and he's deceptively fast. I don't want to say he's taken for granted, but he's always there." Dave Smith says that, as well as looking at refereeing, Troy is weighing offers to play professionally in North America and Europe. "I think he's leaning towards

Europe," he says. "But whatever happens, I'm extremely proud of both of them."

The next morning—it's an 11 o'clock game—Mike Mole records his second shutout in two games as St. FX beats York, 4–0, knocking the Lions out. Afterwards, Sean Murphy says, "Believe or not, I think our team played very well. We got our backs broken [by Dalhousie] when we were up 2–0 and they scored those three quick goals. We had a lot of momentum at the start, hit a couple of goalposts, and I thought that they had trouble getting going and they were down because they'd had that loss (5–0 to St. FX), but those quick goals—it was a team lapse and our goaltender's lapse, and when they beat our goaltender, they beat our strength and we just couldn't recover. As for St. FX, they just flat out just beat us. They were a lot better hockey team than we were. We put up a fight, but it was tough."

UNB is to play Alberta this evening. Five players from Ontario are in the UNB lineup—there would be six, except that last summer twenty-five-year-old Gene Chiarello, a goaltender from Sault Ste. Marie, was diagnosed with cancer. Chiarello played for the London Knights in the OHL. After attending three NHL tryout camps—Chicago, Buffalo and Columbus—and not signing, he decided to go back to school and ended up at UNB. Nowadays, he has no hair because of chemotherapy, and he looks a bit drawn, but he says he feels fine and hasn't lost any weight.

It's between periods of the York–St. FX game, and Chiarello doesn't mind talking about his illness. Sitting in the empty UNB dressing room, he says, "I woke one morning in the middle of July with blurred vision. When it didn't go away in a few days,

I went to an eye doctor, and then I had an MRI and they discovered a growth in my head." He had surgery in Toronto that September. "There was a lot of optimism after it," he says. "[The doctor] had taken out everything that he could and he was confident that it was benign and the vision was corrected."

However, six weeks later, the pathology came back and showed otherwise. The part of the tumor that doctors hadn't been able to reach was not benign at all. Chiarello began chemo in November 2003—his treatments take place at Toronto General Hospital. "It's not like standard chemo, where you might go once a week for three or four hours," he says. "I'm hooked up to IV bags for twenty-four hours [a day], three weeks straight. I get a two-week rest, then it's back for another three weeks. Apart from the hair loss, I feel okay. I see a lot of people in hospital who really suffer side effects. I'm fortunate that I haven't."

Chiarello is out of school for now, living at home in the Soo. A benefit hockey game was held last fall between UNB and the University of Moncton in hopes of raising $10,000 to help pay for his commute to Toronto; it netted more than $19,000. "The support and generosity my family and I have had from the people of Fredericton has just been overwhelming," he says. This is Chiarello's second visit to UNB this season. "You know, almost half the team is new this year, but when I came down in late January they really embraced me," he says. "When I left four days later, I still felt like I was really part of the team." And he hopes to play again. "Absolutely, I'll play," he says. "I wouldn't consider it a full recovery unless I could play hockey again."

In the second game, UNB pulls the upset of the college year, beating favored Alberta 6–5 on a goal four minutes into overtime. This after Alberta had been leading 4–2 early in the third. "We blew this game, period," a sour Rob Daum, the Alberta coach, says afterwards.

Forty service personnel from the Canadian Forces base in nearby Gagetown are here to help with arena security. They're in camouflage battle dress and wouldn't look out of place in Bosnia. When UNB scores the winning goal, a young private has trouble suppressing a cheer and smothering his smile. "You see, sir, we're not meant to show favoritism," he says, "but I'm from Atlantic Canada, too—Newfoundland."

The result means that the best Alberta can do now is a bronze medal. UNB and St. FX will meet for the gold tomorrow night. Jeff Andrews and Gene Chiarello are quietly ecstatic. "One to go," Andrews says.

Among the hockey VIPs here is Clare Drake, who coached the University of Alberta for nearly thirty years. He's seventy-five now, but looks young and fit, and he'd likely bristle at being called a VIP. But he's one of the most respected men in Canadian university hockey and, for those who really know their hockey, likely one of the most respected in the game.

The morning after Alberta's loss, Drake is having breakfast in the hotel dining room. He's disappointed over the game, particularly as Alberta was favored to win it all, but he perks up over his poached eggs. Drake coached the Golden Bears from 1959–60 until 1989–90, the period when university hockey began to come of age. He was also co-coach with Tom Watt (later the coach of the Maple Leafs) and Lorne Davis of the Canadian Olympic team that went to Lake Placid in 1980, and he has taken half a dozen or so Canadian teams to Europe. "I guess it works out to about twenty-nine years at Alberta," he says. Along the way, there was one season, 1975–76, when he was head coach of the Edmonton Oilers in the World Hockey Association.

"That Edmonton experience wasn't very positive," Drake says. "They were a professional team, but they didn't have a lot of professional players, if you know what I mean. It was the early days of the WHA and it was a mixed bag—some really class, quality guys. The first guy who comes to mind is Normie Ullman, who was a great player in the NHL and then came to the WHA. But there were guys with pretty shaky [hockey] backgrounds. I was trying to institute things, and their attitude was, 'Who's this smart-assed college guy?' So we had a real mix; half, I'd say, were really great, and the other half . . . I'm not saying that they were bad people, it's that they needed to change their habits, and they didn't want to."

And then there were two years as an assistant under Bob Murdoch with the Winnipeg Jets. "They were a more professional organization," Drake says, although he points out that this was fourteen years later and, unlike the young Oilers, the Jets were an established team. "The players were quite professional. A couple of them were old school, but most of them were willing to listen and try new things, and because of that they improved."

Then he turns to life after coaching and quotes his old friend Watt, whom he coached against when Watt was behind the bench for the University of Toronto. "Tom's with Anaheim, doing player development. Now and then I bump into him, and he says that he wants to stay in hockey and that old coaches can always become scouts, but they've got to be prepared to sit in cold rinks and watch about 250 games a year, which is not his idea of a good time. That's about the way I feel."

Any scouting Drake does now, he says, he does almost as a favor. "I don't do it very often, but I know a lot of people around the league and someone'll call and say 'Clare, we got a game coming up with Nashville, or whoever, and they're coming in to play Edmonton. Would you go and give us a few thoughts on them?' Stuff like that, but I don't do it much."

Drake says the university game has changed even in the fifteen years since he left it. "Back then, you might have three or four guys from the WHL," he says. "Now the WHL is doing a better job at keeping them in school—but because they're ineligible for NCAA, that leaves the Canadian schools. I have mixed feelings about that because it limits the chances of our Tier II juniors getting Canadian scholarships."

Of his coaching days, he says, "Hockey is no different than anything else, in that learning never stops. And you must be able to motivate your players, give them confidence. And you must tell your veteran players to go all out at tryouts and practice. You want the rookies to see them and say, 'Gee, that's what I have to do to make this team.' Sometimes you'll have kids with all the desire in the world, but not the skills. Other times, desire can keep a kid on a team. You just never know. I wasn't player-friendly. I didn't want to be their buddy. Players must accept discipline—smart discipline, not dumb discipline. We know what smart discipline is."

As an example of bad discipline, Drake tells the story of a player who came to the Golden Bears from the Western Hockey League. "He'd led the WHL in penalty minutes; in fact, he'd set a record. But he was an intelligent boy, quite capable of going to university. As he was trying out for us and in the early games, he was doing the things he'd been doing in the WHL—kept taking penalties, got into fights, was thrown out of games. Finally, I had to tell him that he wasn't going to stick with the team if he stayed with his old habits. He had a tough time changing, but he did change, and a year later he was one of our most valuable players—and the year after that was on our national championship team.

"And sometimes I use 'smart tough' and 'dumb tough.' Being 'smart tough' is playing the game really hard, physically, within the rules. I always used to tell my players that if they want to give a solid check, it hurts a lot more if you get your shoulder into him than get your elbow up or your stick up. Dumb tough is running around taking a lot of dumb penalties and people think you're tough and say, 'Look at that guy; wow, he's tough, isn't he?' And he's ready to drop his gloves, fight anytime. That's dumb tough, at any level. It's just like in the NHL. They get to the playoffs, and they don't use any 'dumb tough' players."

Drake singles out the late Roger Neilson as a great teacher. "He moved around a lot, but because he could teach he was a valuable commodity," he says. He contrasts him with the equally much-traveled Mike Keenan and his reputation for toughness. "He might get a veteran team moving," Drake says. "At least for a while, anyway."

Like many hockey people today, regardless of their age, Drake wonders about the state of the game. But the first thing he mentions is not whether there should be a red line, or whether the ice surface should be larger, or some of the other trimmings. "I think a lot of people are looking at the NHL now and maybe telling themselves that they aren't interested any-more," he says. "There's the violence and the general lack of respect that players have for each other. I've seen parents who are reluctant to steer their kids that way for that reason."

And there is also the cost—in some cases, up to $8,000 a season for a pre-teen or early teenager to play, once registration fees, equipment, travel and insurance are taken into account.

While Drake is finishing his breakfast, Martone and several members of the St. FX team are going for a walk. Martone says he doesn't think anyone went to the optional skate earlier that morning. There'll be a team meeting later, but he doesn't expect anything dramatic. "I guess it'll be just like going into any game," he says.

That afternoon, Alberta loses again, 4–1 to Dalhousie, in the bronze-medal game. Unless you're a Dalhousie fan—a number of them are here from Halifax, and they're thrilled—the game is just a sideshow. Most of the others, this being Fredericton, are looking forward to one thing: the championship game tonight between their beloved UNB Varsity Reds and the St. FX X-Men.

As far as Alberta goes, after what happened against New Brunswick the night before, the bronze-medal game is worse than anticlimactic, it's meaningless. It's almost embarrassing for them to have to play it, considering they'd been favored to win it all. "We played our whole season for last night's game, and we were emotionally drained," coach Rob Daum, never a believer in bronze-medal games, says afterwards. "I don't want to take anything away from Dalhousie, but maybe because of the expectations we had, a win today meant more to them."

That night, it's raining again. Ninety minutes before the game's 7:30 start, the huge parking lot behind the Aitken Centre is almost full. A dozen or so slicker-clad security guards are directing the bumper-to-bumper traffic that's trying to find space.

Outside the rink, a few dozen people are standing in the wet, hands cupped around cigarettes, trying to keep them dry. A couple of hardy souls with pushcarts are selling ribbons in university colors—red and black for UNB, blue and white for St. FX.

Just inside, students are giving out, free of charge and also in university colors, Thundersticks—the inflatable vinyl rods that come in pairs and, when banged together, make cracking sounds loud enough to be the envy of Thor. Nearly 4,000 people are already in their seats or pushing their way in. Scattered throughout the crowd, in small groups, are students, boys and girls, faces painted in their school colors; some of the boys are stripped to the waist, their upper bodies painted. But although it's a loud and fiercely partisan crowd, they're all having a good time.

It's hard to get a fan breakdown because the noise, with the Thundersticks leading the way, is almost nonstop. But when UNB scores twice within five minutes in the first period to take a 2–0 lead, the hometown crowd reacts as if they'd already won the game. That's the way the period ends. The serviceman from Newfoundland, at his post at an entrance at one end of the rink, has his game face back on—the face that doesn't play favorites. Down below, in the VIP lounge, Jeff Andrews and Gene Chiarello take a between-periods break for a pop or beer. They've both played enough hockey to know it's far from over.

Up in the lounge above the ice, watching the game on closed-circuit TV and drinking beer, are three U of Ottawa players: Jeff Pont, Mathieu Blanchard and Dylan Bliss. Their team was eliminated on Friday when they lost to UNB, 5–2—they'd already lost 7–3 to Alberta—but they're still here on Sunday because they aren't booked to fly out until tomorrow. If they were upset about their team's performance they're over it, though they're a bit restless and feel that they're overstaying their welcome. But as Pont puts it, "At the hotel, we can get whatever we want to eat."

Pont is from Revelstoke, B.C., one of five British Columbia natives with the team. He's a forward who played Tier II junior for Chilliwack in the BCHL before attending Ottawa, and although he's not crazy about Ontario, "it's either be there or at the [lumber] mill back home, like everybody else." He's taking social science and has three more years to go. "You work hard, but the rest is fun," he says

Blanchard, a goalie, is from St. Ambroise, Quebec, near Chicoutimi. He played for Hawkesbury in the Central Junior A league before coming to the U of Ottawa. The third member of the trio, Dylan Bliss, is a defenseman from Napanee, Ontario. He was with the Tier II Kingston Voyageurs before university.

Ottawa was the tournament's fourth seed, but Pont, Blanchard and Bliss acknowledge that their team was out of its depth. And looking down the other lineups, it's not hard to see why. For example, only six players on the twenty-seven-man Ottawa roster had played major junior, let alone minor pro. UNB has twelve major juniors, and the University of Alberta a whopping twenty-five.

"We didn't have a great tournament, but we never panicked," Blanchard says. "And it was a real adrenaline rush. We saw a lot of good hockey, and we're better for being here, and they were nice guys we played against." Blanchard loves hockey, and after he leaves school—he's studying human kinetics, which he calls "a fancy term for phys ed"—he'd like to play in Finland, France or Germany. "Hockey's gotta be the toughest game to play," he says. "You need the maximum skill."

Bliss, who is studying management, says he's looking forward to the two years of university hockey he has left. This is from a young man who walked away from hockey a few years ago because he was fed up with it. "I started playing when I was three or four, and then when I got to be about seventeen, hockey just wasn't a priority for me anymore," he says. "It had lost its fun, so I stopped playing." But his break lasted only a year. "I missed the guys, the camaraderie, the bus trips, the competition, just playing the game. So I came back, played junior for a couple of years, and then came to university."

Bliss, like his teammate Blanchard, is glad he was at the tournament in spite of the outcome. "We really didn't know what to expect," he says. Then he says that some of the other universities have an easier time recruiting than the Ontario schools. "I know a lot of guys on the east coast who pretty much get all their schooling paid for," he says. "For us, it's a lot tougher. Sometimes we even have to scramble for sticks."

Graham Wise has coached York University since 1987. He played junior for the old Toronto Marlboros and then for Michigan Tech and the University of Toronto. He wasn't part of this talk with the Ottawa kids, but he agrees with Bliss. "The rules are set by CIS, but in Ontario we're more stringent," he says. "In Atlantic Canada they can offer the cost of tuition to an incoming student. We can't—Ontario won't let us. When I'm trying to recruit an OHL player, I'm offering him a good education and a nice scholarship and a nice facility and some bursary money he might get the first year. When Dalhousie is talking to the same kid, it's, 'You come here and we'll pay for your tuition.' We can offer up to $2,500 as long as they maintain a B average. That's it."

Down on the ice, St. FX scores early in the second period and then, even earlier in the third, at the twenty-seven-second mark, they tie it up at 2–2. The period ends with the score still deadlocked, and a ten-minute overtime solves nothing. About eight minutes into the second overtime, St. FX's Blake Robson, the Calgary native, takes a high-sticking penalty. Robson is a five-year veteran of the WHL, where he played with the Ottawa Senators' Marian Hossa and Brenden Morrow of the Dallas Stars. "Geez," a man in a blue and white scarf tells his girlfriend, "if anyone should know better, it's him. It's overtime, for Chrissakes." Again, the hometown crowd senses victory. But St. FX kills off the penalty, and in a stroke of poetic justice, Robson steps out of the penalty box, takes a pass on the fly from Wes Jarvis, and beats the UNB goalie from ten feet out, high on the glove side.

Finally, St. FX has its first national championship. And for Mike Martone and Troy Smith and a couple of others in their last year of eligibility, they've closed out their college hockey careers on a winning note. After embracing their teammates—either cheering or consoling them—the players from both teams meet at center ice and shake hands. Then, the disconsolate UNB team, the sixth and lowest seed, who almost pulled it off, must line up and face St. FX while the awards and medals are handed out.

Ten minutes later, the closing ceremonies are over, and finally UNB is able to leave the ice. The St. FX players stay on, their gold medals around their necks, engulfed by fans, friends and family, including Dave Smith, who puts his arm around his son Troy. Somebody has brought out a box of cigars. They must be a foot long, and everyone lights up. Mike Martone is shaking his head in wonder, smiling and laughing. About all he can say is, "My God, we did it, we won. What a feeling."

Wes Jarvis, who set up the winning goal, says, "This is the first time I've ever won anything like this. We all played so well, and everybody got on so well together. The quality of these guys is unbelievable."

In the middle of it all is Danny Flynn. Like the others, he's smiling broadly. He's also on a cell phone, shouting to be heard over the din. "He's probably recruiting for next year," the man with the white-and-blue scarf tells his girlfriend.

There were celebrations for the team in Antigonish and Halifax. "I've never seen anything like it," Mike Martone said. A few days later, Danny Flynn was off recruiting. His stops included Prince George and Calgary. Martone got married in July and may go back to play in Mississippi. Wes Jarvis took some political science courses at Carleton University in Ottawa and played a lot of golf. He's back in Antigonish in the fall of 2004. Troy and Mike Smith spent the summer working at home and playing summer hockey. In the fall, Mike also returns to Antigonish, while Troy is hoping to play pro.

Index